3 in

3 in 1

Peter Reading

Chatto & Windus
LONDON

Published in 1992 by
Chatto & Windus Ltd
20 Vauxhall Bridge Road
London SW1V 2SA

A CIP catalogue record for this book is available
from the British Library

ISBN 0 7011 3689 8

Diplopic was first published in 1983, *C* in
1984, *Ukulele Music* in 1985, all by Secker & Warburg

Photoset by
Cambridge Composing (UK) Ltd
Cambridge

Printed in Great Britain
by Mackays of Chatham, PLC
Chatham, Kent.

Contents

DIPLOPIC

Optician, I am having Double Visions
to see one thing from two sides. Only
give me a Spectacle and I am delighted.

> – English Phrases for Malay Visitors
> (Vest-Pocket Editions, 1950)

*   *   *

(1) Vulture, aloof on a thermal;
frail flesh is a commodity
to be scavenged.
(2) Vulture, manipulating still-bloody bones
on the white sand;
Poet, ordering the words of a beautiful sonnet
on the bare page.

> – Two Visions
> (after Kokur Niznegorsky)

*   *   *

Is this Thalia and Melpomene, or am I seein double?

> – Eavesdropped
> (in a Greek restaurant)

AT MARSDEN BAY

Arid hot desert stretched here in the early
Permian Period – sand dune fossils
are pressed to a brownish bottom stratum.
A tropical saline ocean next silted
calcium and magnesium carbonates
over this bed, forming rough Magnesian
Limestone cliffs on the ledges of which
Rissa tridactyla colonizes –
an estimated four thousand pairs
that shuttle like close-packed tracer bullets
against dark sky between nests and North Sea.
The call is a shrill 'kit-e-wayke, kit-e-wayke',
also a low 'uk-uk-uk' and a plaintive
'ee-e-e-eeh, ee-e-eeeh'.

Four boys about sixteen years old appear
in Army Stores combat-jackets, one wearing
a Balaclava with long narrow eye-slit
(such as a rapist might find advantageous),
bleached denims rolled up to mid-calf, tall laced boots
with bright polished toe-caps, pates cropped to stubble.
Three of the four are cross-eyed, all are acned.
Communication consists of bellowing
simian ululations between
each other at only a few inches range:
'Gibbo, gerrofforal getcher yaffuga',
also a low 'lookadembastabirdsmon'.

Gibbo grubs up a Magnesian Limestone
chunk and assails the ledges at random,
biffing an incubating kittiwake
full in the sternum – an audible slap.
Wings bent the wrong way, it thumps at the cliff base,

5

twitching, half closing an eye. Gibbo seizes
a black webbed foot and swings the lump joyously
round and round his head. It emits
a strange wheezing noise. Gibbo's pustular pal
is smacked in the face by the flung poultry, yowls,
and lobs it out into the foam. The four
gambol euphoric like drunk chimps through rock pools.
Nests are dislodged, brown-blotched shells crepitate
exuding thick rich orange embryo goo
under a hail of hurled fossilized desert
two hundred and eighty million years old.

EDITORIAL

Being both *Uncle Chummy's Letter Box*
of *Kiddies' Column* and *Supa Scoop* besides
(*Your Headlines As They Happen*), and having the shakes
uncellophaning fags this crapulous morning,
I compose: BOY (13) CLUBS DAD TO DEATH,
CHILD (10) SCALDS GRANNY (87) TO DEATH,
SKINHEAD (14) STONES KITTIWAKES TO DEATH
AS RSPCA ASKS 'WHERE'S THE SENSE?'.

Better this afternoon after the Vaults,
I award 50 pence to Adam (9)
for this: 'Dear Uncle Chummy, I am writing
to let you know about my hamster Charlie
who's my best friend . . .' 'Keep up the good work, kiddies . . .'
(sinister dwarfs, next issue's parricides).

DARK CONTINENT

Big fat essays are being inserted
into resistant pigeon-holes. Chalky,
who once lived in Africa, is giving
the SCR the benefit of
his experience in those parts 'The *Nkonga*
Herald often carried reports
of offences of Chicken Buggery . . .'

Flora Mackenzie (2nd Year English)
has tackled, for her Creative Writing,
the sanguinary 'Death of a Grouse'
(*In crumpled feather wings of prayer*
Heather she lived in, no man harming
She lies and bleeds her rose red root
Her wattle wilted willed to waste
The bird is free, man's lust is caged . . .
etcetera, etcetera; God).

'The Prof's in a bit of a sweat. It seems
he picked up the Departmental Phone
and who should be on the other end
but Mrs Mackenzie – gave him pure Hell,
said Flora's run off with a 3rd Year Mining
Engineering student, a black,
one Bongoman Bulawayo, I think,
to Zimbabwe or somewhere, and she said
"Hoots! Toots! What are ye goin to do, mon?"
Prof said "Your daughter *is* over eighteen."
Well, she flew off the handle, said "Hoots! Toots!
I gave her to you in good faith . . ."'

                                   A rose
finger of dawn caresses a mud hut,
awakens the delicate, shy, pale Flora
(who strains and frets under sleek black thew)
to that Dark Continent, where men
are men, and the poultry is very uneasy.

9

RECEIPT

Unto the stock, that hath been simmering
slowly for nearly twenty-four hours already,
cast ye a bushel of the following, mixed:
shoots of the sacred Ashphodeliaboo,
Roogin, Wormwillow, Auberjelly Lime,
Elephant Quince, Sweet Portalooforago,
Smiley Potatoes, Voodoo Saxifrapple,
verdant Aspariagora, Zulu Froom,
Lily of fragrant Umpo, Virgin's Ice,
a stick of Popgo (black), two sprigs of Kak-Kak.
Marinade dugs, sliced thickly into steaks,
with Shamilee and crushed dried seeds of Xeppit
   (which method served to cook the white poetess
   Flora, 9th wife of the gourmand Bongoman).

THE TERRESTRIAL GLOBE

Señor Garcia
descends a staircase
hopping on one hand.
Three steps down,
not unnaturally,
he sprains his wrist
and sprawls in the sawdust.
He leaps to his feet,
bows, bursts into tears.

Il Maestro subdues
two lionesses,
two Bengal tigresses
and one unidentified
heavily moulting
very male quadruped.

The Brothers Alfonso
perform on stilts.
One of them bears
a striking likeness
to *Señor Garcia*
and, trying to do
'The very difficult
Backward Somersault',
falls on his head.
He removes his stilts,
bows, bursts into tears.

'And now, all the way
from West Germany,'
(a bald Chinese
of ferocious aspect

and droopy moustaches
(flexes her biceps)
'The Strongest Woman
The World Has Known,
Miss Herculess,
will carry *Miss Jill*
in this gigantic
Terrestrial Globe.'
Miss Jill climbs into
the ferrous contraption,
sealed in tight
with a saucer-like lid.
The Chinese raises
the huge sphere until
it is over her head
then hurls it clanging
into the ground.
The audience gasps,
screams come from within.
Anxious hands drag
Miss Jill out to safety,
blood smears her costume.
Miss Herculess shrieks,
first in Cantonese,
then in thick Glaswegian,
'D'ye ken I'm no blind!
Keep awa frae my mon!'

A dromedary
of prodigious age
is chased by two llamas
gratuitously
round several dozen
laps of the Big Top . . .

THE BIG CATS

        bicker. Fodens churn the rec.
into an Auerbach slough. A squat grey bomb
of Calor hisses under a caravan
labelled not only JILL – CONTORTIONIST

but also SEÑOR GARCIA – FABULOUS
MANIPULATOR EXTRAORDINAIRE
and also THE STRONGEST WOMAN KNOWN TO MAN.
Two tigresses tease red skin, suck stiff bone.

Grunts, lately of the jungle, fade to moans.
The lettered van jolts on its springs. Pink bare
meat rises slowly in the steamed-up glass.
Glut, guzzle, slurp, drool, slobber, mumble, snort –

rank felines, scarcely tame, extravasate,
vie to possess inflamed raw purple flesh.

MINIMA

After

      the telegram-boy's purse-lipped dirge,
the slicing open,
the ghastly revelation,

the bereaved Parnassian
hones a canine tooth,
sharpens a pencil.

Epicedium

Ah well, it could be worse – it could be *me*.

TELECOMMUNICATION

    The telegram-boy's little red Suzuki.
The pasted strips TELEPHONE FATHER URGENT.
The feeling trembly, squittery and pukey.
The breakfast things left in the cold detergent.
    The milled edge of a coin on the thumb-pad.
The voice at the other end 'Yes, late last night'.
The feeling scared/exhilarated/numb. Sad
memories of – (enough of all that shite).

    The puny hug, meant to propitiate.
Strong, palliating Fino de Jerez.
The weak reply, meant to initiate
a five-year-old into peculiar Death
    'Yes, Grandma's bones *might* fossilize, of course,
    like those in your *First Book of Dinosaurs*'.

WAR ARTISTES

(There is one of them War Artistes with our lot. He seems not quite human. He drawers even when the heavy firing is on. He done a water colours picture of poor Carew with his head blowed clean off – a very pretty thing, and I don't think! I think he SEES things different to us. – From a letter to his brother, c. 1917, by Thomas Gibb, in the author's possession.)

    We are always out there
       with pencils raised,
  treacherous bastards,
      Double Agents
  not working for *you*
      but for some Secret Power.

    If an awful thing happens,
      we will appear –
  coyotes, dingoes,
      jackals, hyenas,
  lapping up
      universal holocausts.

    We have a horrible
      kind of diplopia –
  (1) straight, clinical,
      accurate, X-ray,
  (2) refracted
      to serve our bent calling.

MNEMONICS

Some matter is too delicate to define
with muted chalks or the restricted palette
implicit in small portable tubes of gouache
(e.g. the whitish-tallows and wax-yellows
and algal-greens of military flesh).
Mnemonics are essential – the best method
is to annotate draft studies in the field
for later more urbane studio finish.

May in the squares is the white of Devon cream,
in the warm sun ripe Georgian brick assumes
the russet of port half a century old.
Ribs bright cream, whitest teeth . . . wrote Kennington
on his dead Jerry (circa 1916)
that hangs now in peaceful Clifford Street, West One.

P.S.

The stitching new on your tiny rectangle of black,
you immerse yourself in the sad therapy of the kitchen,
withdrawing from sight when assailed by trembling and weeping.
I mailed you my useless sympathy but, reticently,
withheld admiration and love for you (old-fashioned words)
who, having a grim chore to finish, get on with the job.

HINTS

Find ways to make the narrative compel,
I advise students; as, in retailing this,
you might lend the issue added poignancy
by being distanced – describe the electrified
overgrown line in cool botanical terms,
white cow-parsley, *Anthriscus sylvestris*,
adding the child with anthropological
detachment, ten years old, print dress, bewildered . . .

Compelling, maybe, but mere narrative –
no moral or intellectual envoy.
Accentuate the dignified resilience
that humans, or some, are capable of still,
evinced in the sad braveness of the bereaved
whose daughter, being blind, observed no warning.

AT HOME

She is nearly 87,
and her house is ten years older.
In the garden huge old beech trees,
silver-boled in winter sunshine,
have the following carved on them
(though the scars are mossed and healed now):
JOHN CAREW L SALLY HIBBERT.
In her chair of woven basket,
in the window-bay with pot-plants,
she drinks Earl Grey every morning,
reads the *Telegraph* and wonders
why young people now are vicious,
disrespectful, stoned and randy.
On her knees a tartan blanket,
in her lap soft-centre bon-bons.
(An interior like that in
Lamb's *Portrait of Lytton Strachey*.)

In a silver cage a mynah
chews a grape and spits the pips out.
In a silver frame a photo
of a young World War I soldier
signed JC in faded sepia.

Carved black elephants, brass kettles
fitted with bright amber handles,
Taj Mahals by moonlight rendered
in bright dyes on thin silk, jewel-
hilted daggers indicate some
past connection with the raj. Dates
gleam in chevrons down a central
spine in a round-ended carton.

* * *

Senior Police Officials
dealing with the case were 'frankly
baffled' as to who could do this.
Supa Scoop's reporter comments:

This is no mere petty break-in.
Here was a defenceless woman,
frail, old, well-liked, partly crippled,
living on her Old Age Pension,
living all alone, her only
company an ageing cage-bird,
scalded, beaten, slashed, hair pulled out,
fingers broken – her assailants
making off (when, quite unable
to supply them information
as to any 'hoard of savings',
she fell at their feet unconscious),
making off with £1.60,
making off with *£1.60*,
making off with £1.60
and a box of CHOCKO YUM-YUMS.

*   *   *

In the tray of sand and faeces
at the bottom of the bird-cage
it spins rhythmically on one wing
where a stump of singed flight-feathers
joins a dislocated shoulder.
All the primaries are burnt off.
It emits a hissing whisper
'Hello sailor, Hello sailor.'
Slowly, nictitating membranes
squeeze across dull-bloomed sclerotics.

*   *   *

When she opened up the front door
Gibbo punched her in the guts like,
give her head-butts, dragged her screamin
into the front room. I says 'Look,
where's yer bleedin money, Mrs?'
She says nuffink so I rubs these
chocolates what she had hard in her
face like. Then we gets this knife thing
what she had hung on the wall like
and we gives her face the old quick
criss-cross with the point. She gives us
all this crap: 'Wah-wah, you demons,
have you no love for your mothers?'
So I gives her hair a bleedin
pull what sent her screamin. It was
dead great, how she screamed and screamed and
how her hair come out in handfuls.
Gibbo gets this bleedin budgie
what she had in this big cage thing
and he got its wings and lit them
with his old fag-lighter. It was
dead great how that parrot-thing went
up in smoke. Gib bit its beak off.
That was dead great, how he done it.
Then we found her purse and all it
had was bleedin one pound fifty
so we give her fingers the old
snap-snap like and Gibbo tells her
'If you don't say where you've got it
hid, I'll give ya boilin water.'
And he did. That was dead great like.
There was dates – I don't like them much.

MYNAH PETRARCHAN*

What a big fellow *he* is for his age!
Give us a drink. I likes a drop of rum.
Hello there, sailor boy! Who loves his mum?
Look at that bird! Let's stuff it full of sage
and onion! Cocky's out on the rampage!
Everyone loves black Cocky! Give us some!
Cocky's a wicked naughty! Smack his bum!
Cocky likes nice boys. Lock him in his cage.

Cocky must stay inside. Sit on his perch.
Speak to me, Cocky. Say a little wordie.
Give us a kiss, then. Who's a pretty boy?
What would poor mummy do left in the lurch?
What if the bad boys got her little birdie?
Where would she be without her pride and joy?

---

* Declaimed by Oriental passerine.

AFTER SANRAKU KOSHU

Jailed for being drunk,
but far from contrite, the bard,
minus shoes, tie, belt,
savoured steel grille, rank pallet,
mused 'Ah! Raw Material!'

SORTIE

'Didn't you hear about it? Well, as planned, he
went up to Town and lunched quite well at Wheeler's
– Pol Roger '71 with half a dozen
large Irish oysters, fine bottle of Clicquot
'75 with a dressed lobster, '60
Dow's with a Stilton. Looked up "Stinker"'s cousin,
drank '63 Warre's with him at the Savile,
then on to "Stinker"'s for Cockburn's '45.
Caught, by mistake, a train to Crewe, where Peelers
found him in deep repose (fatigued by travel
and tiny phials of Inter-City brandy).
Night spent in durance vile. Next day the beak – "Oh,
tell me, are you drunk frequently?". He fixed the
ass with a scowl and got quite haughty – "I've
never touched Strong Drink (but for a Christmas Fino)."
£10. Quite an amusing little beano.'

15TH FEBRUARY

I tried to put in what I really felt.
I really tried to put in what I felt.
I really felt it – what I tried to put.
I put it really feelingly, or tried.
I felt I really tried to put it in.
What I put in I tried to really feel.
Really I felt I'd tried to put it in.
I really tried to feel what I put in.

It cost £5 in WH Smith's.
£5 it cost – WH Smith's ain't cheap.
£5 ain't cheap, not for a thing like that.
It costs, a thing like that – £5 ain't cheap.
It wasn't a cheap thing – £5 it cost.
A thing like that ain't cheap in WH Smith's.
In WH Smith's a thing like that comes costly.
A lot to pay, £5, for a thing like that.

The heart was scarlet satin, sort of stuffed.
I sort of felt it was me own heart, like.
SHE TORE THE STUFFING OUT OF THE SCARLET HEART.
I sort of stuffed and tore her sort of scarlet.
I stuffed her, like, and felt her sort of satin.
I sort of felt she'd tore out all me stuffing.
I felt her stuff like satin sort of scarlet
her stuff felt sore, torn satin whorlet scar
I liked her score felt stiffed her scar lick hurt
I tore her satin felt her stuffed her scarlet
tore out her heart stuff scarred her Satan har
I licked her stiff tore scarf her harlot hair
tied scarf tore stabbed scar whore sin sat tit star
stuffed finger scar ha ha ha ha ha ha
felt stiff scarf tight tore scarlet heart her scare
her scare stare stabbed heart scarlet feel torn mur

FOUND

Strange find – a plastic dummy from a boutique
(boots, white long thighs, pants pulled right down, a sack
over the head and torso) dumped among bins
and tumps of fetid garbage and coils of rank
sloppy dog faeces in an ill-lit alley
between the Launderette and Indian Grocer.
Incorrect diagnosis: it emits
a high-pitched rattle like Callas gargling.

Rescrutinizing 36 hours later:
what was, in sodium light, viridian,
is, in pale February sun, maroon.
About a soup-cupful remains still viscous,
black at the rim where a scabbed mongrel sniffs,
ripples taut sinew, salivates and laps.

STEDMAN'S

I am going to write a sonnet
concerning Huntington's Chorea
from the viewpoint of a Year 2
Pharmacy student, and so
I am looking up **Chorea** in
Stedman's Medical Dictionary.

On the same page as I require,
this appears: **Choreophrasia** –
*The continual repetition
of meaningless phrases.*

               I wonder
if I ought, after all, to dispatch
the pharmacist's Granny by means of
convulsions, or whether to have her
reduced to a jabbering night-hag
whose terminal speech* could be rendered
with agreeable anarchy.

   *   Carew, Carew, Carew, my bonny lad.
Where do we go from here? Brisk cockatoo.
Happy the man who knows not he is glue.
Which way? Which way? I *love* Jahanabad
in Spring. What drunken bard? An ironclad
means tank. My bonny lad. Carew, Carew.
From here we venture to the Portaloo
of death. Brisk cockatoo is very bad!
     I had a Polly budgie in a box.
Seagull and fox. Paisley is *not* OK.
Carew, Carew, Carew, cock, cocky, cocky.
These sweets are jolly fudgy. Chicken Pox!
These literary magazines are fey,
cock, cocky, cock. Carew. I hates a trochee!

In *A Sort of Life*, Greene remarked
(mitigating the relish with which
he observed parental distress
at the death of a ten-year-old)
'There is a splinter of ice
in the heart of a writer.'

                            I savour
the respective merits of one
kind of mayhem over another,
contentedly ponder the species
of fourteen-liner most apposite –
Petrarchan? Elizabethan?

A RECOLLECTION

She always was a great one for the pranks.
We hadn't seen her for about 5 years.
To find her in that place with all those cranks
was like one of her jokes – we laughed till our tears
unfocused her as she winked, twitched and flexed
her limbs. Then we saw that she was weeping too,
realized the reason for the high-walled, annexed,
discreetly-labelled building.

                      Sleeping through
most of the morning's 2nd Year Pharmacy,
he emerged drowsily, heard, as in a dream,
'. . . Huntington's Chorea. Though, when calmer, she
exhibited no more symptoms than extreme
involuntary twitching . . .' and recalled
the childhood visit and was newly appalled.

NIPS

Look at the high tor!
The rocks are older than men
and will last longer.

Thank you very much
for pointing this out to us,
PBS Spring Choice.

                    *   *   *

Crossing the campus
with a 6 by 6 canvas
in a force 7,
the art student looks like a
discomfited Wright brother.

His large oil depicts
a seagull in a tweed suit
boxing with a fox
who wears muffler and flat cap.
(An allegory, I think.)

                    *   *   *

Touching to see men
normally at variance
unite (in whining
about meagre salaries
at the Faculty Meeting).

                    *   *   *

31

The Prime Minister
is an incompetent fool,
Rustics are bumpkins,
Townies are corrupt. I am
a good man and know what's what.

* * *

In last week's press, X
reviewed Y: *One of the best
poets now writing.*

In this week's press, Y
reviews X: *One of the best
poets writing now.*

* * *

Not Nell Gwynn (alas),
but the <u>intense</u>, short, hirsute
editor of *Stand*
importunes our theatre queue –
'Come! Buy my juicy lit. mags!'

Phoney-rustic bards,
spare us your thoughts about birds,
butterflies, fish, snakes
and mammals (including us)
– biologists write more sense.
Down the lab they think
these crows, peasants, pikes, eels, swifts
are twee, ill-observed.

Bumpkins, from whose bums
you consider the sun shines,
think you're townee twits.
Like that haiku frog,
unscientific fauna
is a bore in verse.

EX LAB

I

Dilute acetic
has exposed from the matrix
(limestone, Jurassic),
ischium and ilium
and interlocking pubis.

These demonstrate how
ornithischian hip-joints
differ from those of
saurischians. These bits are
believed. *Scelidosaurus.*

After coffee-break
they will be made ready for
hardening resin.
 These flimsy inked surfaces
 come from the Late Holocene:

 CIRCUS STRONG-WOMAN
 CONVICTED OF MANSLAUGHTER.
 STUDENT 'GOES MISSING'
 IN AFRICAN MYSTERY.
 SKINHEAD SETS FIRE TO CAGE-BIRD.

In what was Dorset
one hundred and eighty five
million years ago,
Megalosaurus et al
flenched, flensed these bastards to mince.

II

I am cleaning up
a piece of dinosaur shit
(Upper Cretacious,
length 20 centimetres)
that came from Mongolia.

Someone else requires
the air-abrasive machine
urgently. I stop
and peruse my copy of
a Nietzsche biography.

Up to a point, yes.
'God is dead' – quite straightforward.
But why, then, go on
to think some mitigation
is needed for us to face

Godless cosmic dust?
Matter just gets on with it.
Saying 'YES to life',
conceiving 'Übermenschen'
is an arrogant sell-out

quite as fey as 'God'.
Anyway, Nietzsche was nuts –
got stopped by the fuzz
for taking off his clothing
and bathing in a puddle.

This one matrix holds
fragments of eggshell (believed
Protoceratops –
about ninety million years
of age) and a turd fossil.

I believe in this:
no Übermenschen's remnant
(not one coprolite)
is going to be better
than this elegant stone crap.

III

       Is Sin Sinful*ness?*
       preoccupies my pious
       colleagues over lunch.
Hydrogen and Helium –
the Original Sinners.

On this diagram
(chrono-stratigraphical),
3.6 billion
years ago may be seen as
about the start of Earth life.

       When your daughter dies
       aged ten, mown down by a train,
       console yourself thus:
       sky-pilots can forgive her
       by saying a Special Thing.

On this diagram,
the Holocene or Recent
(last ten thousand years)
is far, far, far, far too small
to register on this scale.

> You live, then you die.
> This is extremely simple.
> You live, then you die –
> no need to wear funny hats,
> no need for mumbo-jumbo.

IV

The '62 find,
Heterodontosaurus
(southern Africa,
Upper Trias), concerned me
greatly because of the *teeth*

(rather than because
Scelidosaurus had been
the earliest known
ornithischian till then)
– that almost 'canine' 'eye-tooth'!

> Oozing bonhomie,
> we take unwanted nick-nacks
> to the Oxfam shop –
> at last! the starving millions
> will have a nice bite to eat!

The stomach contents
of an *Anatosaurus*
I am working on
were mummified – pine-needles
seventy million years old.

In Belfast, I read,
the craze is for hunger-strikes.
Eat your porridge up
like good little murderers
(Political Status, balls).

These five gastroliths
(stomach-stones to grind food) were
worn smooth as pool balls
by an unknown sauropod
of the Upper Jurassic.

Called to specialize
in one stratigraphical
field, I decided
the Late Holocene (*our* scene)
did not concern me greatly.

V

At the end of the
Cretacious, a 'Great Dying'
seems to have occurred,
when half of all animal
and plant groups became extinct.

That extinction seems
to have been protracted for
a few million years;
this one, now underway, will
have reached a similar scale

in a few decades.
The hiatus resulting
in some processes
of evolution will be
extremely fascinating.

      'SUPER-TANKA SINKS'
      (the mis-print suggests Baroque,
      fugal, cumbersome
      development of the Five-
      Seven-Five-Seven-Seven . . .).

What one enjoys most
is the manipulation
of these hapless things
at such impartial distance
to fit an imposed order.

Of course one does not
really care for the *objects*,
just the *subject*. It
is a Vulture Industry,
cashing-in on the corpses.

Vacuum, cosmic dust,
algae, rhipidistians,
internecine us
(it is a fucking good job
that it all does not matter).

FROM A JOURNAL
(c. 1917, in the author's possession)

My Grandfather knew Gideon Algernon Mantell
(discoverer of the Iguanodon*)*
who shewed him, in 1822, in Sussex,
those teeth! of creatures hitherto undreamed-of.

My Grandfather, in 1841,
was at the B.A.A.S. Plymouth meeting*
when Doctor (later Prof., Sir) Richard Owen
unleashed the Dinosaur on smug Victorians.

My Grandfather, a polymath, drew well,
botanized, 'Englished' Vergil, geologized.
My Grandfather was born in 1800,
Father in 1850, I myself
in 1895 . . .

He would have been
88 (but for 1917).

---

* At the 1841 Plymouth meeting of the British Association for the
Advancement of Science, Owen (1804–1892), first Director of the Natural
History Museum in South Kensington, suggested that *Iguanodon, Megalo-*
saurus and *Hylaeosaurus* should together be named the Dinosauria, the
'terrible lizards'.

ENGLISHED (ii. 458)

Far from the clash of Celt twerps,
        the Barley Mow telly transmits
atrocities none of the rustics
        attends to lest they eclipse
his own catalogue of woes –
        the price of bag-muck increases,
Hill Subsidies insufficient
        to run the Merc and the Rover.

The muggings, the dole queues, the miners
        (audaciously asking for more)
are ignored; the new Combine is costing
        (Nat-West) 46 grand,
masonry bees are molesting
        the Georgian brick of the Glebe.
Salopian swains make merry
        with rough rhymes and boisterous mirth.

O fortunatos nimium,
        sua si bona norint . . .
– farmers are fortunate fuckers,
        wanting the wit to know it.

(Shropshire, July 1981)

ENGLISHED (iii.349–83)

Winter is simply beastly for northern neatherds,
girt in the smelly pelts of Reynard and Ursa,
crouched in uncomfy igloos killing time swilling
gassy cyder and frothy Bass and frolicking.

Boreas's eastern child whines incessantly.
You could drive your muck-spreader on the icèd tarn.
The kine are all dead and under 7 cubits
of snow. The antlery tribes are stuck numb in drifts.

Your duds freeze stiff as you stand by the elm log blaze.
Brazen nick-nacks from Brum burst asunder with cold.
Icicles crackle in uncombed hairies' beavers.
It's really really rotten to be Rhyphaean.

Oenophiles give you Grands Crus by weight, not volume,
cleaving the frozen Lafite with their tomahawks.

(Tyne & Wear, January 1982)

EPITHALAMIUM

I

. . . have great pleasure in . . .
of their daughter Crystal . . .
enclosed Gift List . . .

> Dragonstraw door mat in plaited seagrass
> from China.
> 'Tik Tok' wall clock, battery operated
> quartz movement in pine frame.
> 'La Primula Stripe' dishwasher-proof
> glazed earthenware coffee set.
> Valance with neat box pleats to fit
> 3ft to 5ft beds (fixed by Velcro pads).
> Michel Guérard's kitchen work table
> with base of solid pine, including
> a duckboard shelf for storage,
> a knife rack and pegs for teacloths.
> Boxwood pastry crimper.
> 'Confucius' 50% polyester,
> 50% cotton duvet cover.
> Pine wine rack.
> Pine lavatory paper holder.
> Solid pine toilet seat with chrome fittings
> (coated with 6 layers of polyurethane).
> Iron omelette pan with curved sides.
> Angus Broiler cast iron pan for steaks
> and chops which combines the ease of frying
> with the goodness of grilling.
> 'Leonardo' sofa in cream herringbone.
> Honey-coloured beech bentwood rocker
> with cane back and seat.
> Cork ice-bucket with aluminium insert.
> 'Mr Toad' rattan chair from France.
> Tough cotton canvas Sagbag filled
> with flame-retardant polystyrene granules.

II

The fizz is Spanish, labelled 'MEGOD CHAMPAIN'.

III

. . . have great pleasure in . . .
will now read Greetings Cards . . . .

> de da de da de da de da this wedding gift to you
> de da de da de da de da your golden years come true . . .
> All the way from America . . .
> sorry can't be there . . .
> would love to have been there . . .
> a California 'Howdy!' . . .
> de da de da de da de da all your hopes and fears
> de da de da de da de da throughout the coming years . . .

HA HA HA HA HA HA HA (what a riot the Best Man *is*).

IV

At their new home – 'Crimmond' (next to 'Sinatra' on one side
and 'Mon Rêve' on the other) – the presents are laid out.
They look lovely, don't they, Confucius, Leonardo and Mr
Toad.

V

Bog paper and boots are tied to their bumper.
Consummation in Calais is nothing to write home about.

CARTE POSTALE

Dear Mum and Dad,
                            The picture shows a 'gendarme'
which means policeman. France is overrated.
For two weeks it has been wet. 9th September:
we had a 'dégustation' in the Côte
de Mâconnais and Mal got quite light-headed.
Sometimes I think it will be *too* ideal
living with Mal – it's certainly the Real
Thing. I must go now – here comes Mal.
                                      Love, Crystal.

Encircling her slim waist with a fond arm,
the husband of a fortnight nibbles her throat,
would be dismayed to learn how she had hated
that first night when in Calais he had kissed all
over her, and, oh God!, how she now dreaded
each night the importunate mauve-capped swollen member.

BETWEEN THE HEADLINES

(Not if she knew her X-ray result.)
STAR QUITS HOSPITAL CURED

(Not acrimonious veg
but internecine Celts.)
GREENS CLASH WITH ORANGES

*(Not like a mongrel picking up spare bones,
I try to photograph wars with compassion
opines McCullin* on purveying mayhem.)*
BABY SHOT IN BELLY

(Not democratic: on Election Day,
soldiers, the oldest of them about 15,
dispose of corpses at the polling booths
then resume licking their lollipops.)
30,000 CIVILIANS CLAIMED

(Not nice Nips send huge
vessel containing crude-oil
to drive imported
Yamahas and Suzukis
and bugger up your beaches.)
SUPER TANKA SINKS – SLICK SLAYS SEAGULLS

(Not had such a supper in their life
and the little ones chewed on the bones-o
bones-o
bones-o
not had such a supper in their life
and the little ones chewed on the bones-o.)
STUDENT 'GOES MISSING' IN AFRICAN MYSTERY

* Declared by *Newsweek* 'the greatest battlefield photographer of our time'.

(Not-Foreskin v Foreskin –
Old Testament berks
in daft dressing-gowns
and peep-toe slippers
play atavistic
grenade-lobbing pranks
in the Holy Land.)

SALAAM/SHALOM SHAM

(Not to be regarded
as more than a physiological
characteristic – a big brain
does not mean specific aloofness.
Don't think *thinking* makes you
different from, say, rhipidistians.
Souls/arse-holes are the same stuff
– very thin stripes in a tall cliff.)

PORTALOO CLAIMS FOSSIL PROF

ADMISSIONS

Both were unconscious on arrival, one
with serious head injuries, the other
with broken back and ribs and damaged pelvis
(they were put with the factory accident
who'd been admitted earlier with a severed
arm, only 16, he died later too).
Both had been injured when a lorry shed
its load of Portaloo site-lavatories
impartially on a bus queue. One of them,
a circus tightrope-walker, sat bolt upright,
bowed, burst into floods of tears and then expired
wheezing 'Miss Jill! Miss Jill! Miss Jill!'. The other,
a palaeontologist, died screaming out
'THE HOLOCENE DID NOT CONCERN ME GREATLY!'.

FINDS

1

The *Mammuthus*, winched from the permafrost
during the famous Schmitstein expedition
of '51, was truly magnificent,
the finest-preserved specimen yet found –
tusks 4.8 m, 3.3 at shoulder.

It was transported, carefully supervised
by scientists from the Ghustphsen Institute,
back to the base at Skruskhev where impromptu
laboratory facilities were installed.

One of the expedition's porters owned
a husky of unprepossessing aspect.
One night it gained admission to the lab
and ate the 20,000 year-old trunk.

II

The Schneider had one 75 mm
gun, also two machine guns. Double armour
plates on the front, the sides and top. These plates
were separated with a 1.5
inch space between them. Armour varied from
.2 inches to .95 inches.
Maximum speed about 5 miles per hour.
Vertical coil springs, jointed bogie frames.
Tracks – solid plates with single grousers, width
was 14 inches, pitch 10 inches. Length
19 feet 8, width 6 feet 7, height
7 feet 10. Weight 14.9 tons.
A Schneider 70 horse-power water-cooled

4 cylinder engine. There were sliding gears,
3 forward, 1 reverse. Range – 25
miles on a fuel tank holding 53
gallons. Equipped with double tailpiece. Nose
intended as wire-cutter and to assist
in crossing obstacles. Unditching beam
carried on right side. Dome ventilating louvre
on top of hull. The overhanging hull
greatly reduced rough-ground mobility.
Vertical armour plates could not withstand
the celebrated German bullet the 'K'.

A nasty versifier is researching,
sniffing historic carnage, adding salt . . .

RESOLUTION

When the French tank the *Schneider* was introduced
(capable of 6 kilometres per hour,
weight 15 tons, guns 75 mm)
in the bright April sun of '17,
a subaltern watched two tree-pipits ascend
from the black jagged shelled limbs of a pine
and entered sundry commonplaces in this
journal – concluding with the desultory

Watched pipits' song-flight. Saw new ironclad
capable of 6 kilometres per hour,
weight 15 tons, guns 75 mm.
Tonight, after lights-out, I am resolved,
although I love you, Sally, to lie brow-down
on a grenade and then to detonate it.

TRYST

Me and Gib likes it here – always comes of a night,
no one else gets here, see. That's his Great-Grandad's stone.
Gassed, *he* was; got sent home from one of them *old* wars.
        Tommy, they called him.

We sprayed HARTLEPOOL WANKERS on one of them.
                                  Great!
  This is the newest one – sad it is, really, it's
some little ten-year-old girlie's. Them plastic daffs
        look very nice, though.

He likes to get me down in the long weeds between
two of them marble things – I can see ivy sprout
on the cross by his head. He makes me squiggle when
        he sticks his hand up.

He works at one of them mills what makes cattle food.
He stacks the sacks. You should see them tattoos on his
arms when he flexes them. There is a big red heart
        with TRUE LOVE on it.

He runs the Packer-thing all on his own, he does.
We're saving up to get married and have a big
do like that big snob that works in our office had
        (Crystal, her name is).

I let him do what he wants – he pretends that he's
the Ripper, sometimes, and gets me down on a grave;
then what he does with his hands feels like scurrying
        rats up my T-shirt.

When we've saved up enough, we're going to wed in church.
This is alright, though – at least in the summertime.
They don't pay poor Gib much, stacking them heavy sacks
                    off the conveyor.

PACEPACKER

THE *PACEPACKER* NEEDS ONE OPERATOR ONLY.
PLACE EMPTY PAPER SACKS IN RACK MARKED 'SACKS',
ENSURING THEY ARE CLAMPED TIGHT WITH SPRING CLAMP.
ADJUST CONVEYORS TO CORRECT HEIGHTS. SWITCH ON.
WHEN 'START RUN' LIGHT SHOWS GREEN, PRESS 'START RUN'
                                                    BUTTON.
SACKS ARE PICKED UP BY SUCKERS, STITCHED AND CONVEYED
TO ELEVATOR. ENSURE CLOTHING AND HANDS
ARE CLEAR OF CONVEYOR BELT.

                          The corrugated
rapidly-moving strip of rubber seemed
to draw the arm smoothly, unresistingly
up through the oiled steel rollers. The 'Stop Run' light
shows red. The matt belt glistens where a smear
of pink mulch, fatty lumps, flensed skin, singed hair,
is guzzled dry by plump impartial houseflies.

C

*(Incongruously I plan
100 100-word units.)*

The brass plate polished wordless. Stone steps hollowed by the frightened hopeful ascending, the terrified despairing descending. (Probably between three and four months, perhaps one hundred days.) Out of the surgeries in this Georgian street, and similar streets in similar cities, some of us issue daily, bearing the ghastly prognostications. How we hate you, busy, ordinary, undying – taxi-driver, purveyor of the *Evening Star*, secretary bouncing puddings of malleable flesh. Incongruously I plan 100 100-word units. What do you expect me to do – break into bloody haiku?

> Verse is for healthy
> arty-farties. The dying
> and surgeons use prose.

* * *

The *Whale* is situated on the quay and is used by ferrymen and travellers calling for a quick drink before crossing. The *Colliers* is frequented by men from the pit. The fellow known as Tucker regularly attends both establishments. Perhaps he is in charge of the turnstile, the palm of his hand constantly grey from receiving pennies. Or he may be a gypsy, for he deals, apparently, in horses. He addressed me one evening in the bar of the *Whale* with importunate familiarity, remarking that I might henceforward know him as 'Char' (short for 'Charlie'?) or 'Mort' (short for 'Mortimer'?).

* * *

McGill-Melzack Pain Questionnaire word descriptors for scoring methods:

Flickering, Quivering, Pulsing, Throbbing, Beating, Pounding, Jumping, Flashing, Shooting, Pricking, Boring, Drilling, Stabbing. Lancinating, Sharp, Cutting, Lacerating, Pinching, Pressing, Gnawing, Cramping, Crushing, Tugging, Pulling, Wrenching, Hot, Burning, Scalding, Searing, Tingling, Itchy, Smarting, Stinging, Dull, Sore, Hurting, Aching, Heavy, Tender, Taut, Rasping, Splitting, Tiring, Exhausting, Sickening, Suffocating, Fearful, Frightful, Terrifying, Punishing, Gruelling, Cruel, Vicious, Killing, Wretched, Blinding, Annoying, Troublesome, Miserable, Intense, Unbearable, Spreading, Radiating, Penetrating, Piercing, Tight, Numb, Drawing, Squeezing, Tearing, Cool, Cold, Freezing, Nagging, Nauseating, Agonizing, Dreadful, Torturing.

Present Pain Intensity (PPI) intensity scale:

No Pain, Mild, Discomforting, Distressing, Horrible, Excruciating.

* * *

Disseminated spinal carcinoma.
I have lost all control and movement of
the abdomen, legs, feet and back. The growth
(particularly painful) on the spine
prevents my lying on my back. Bedsores
daily increase in size, restrict still more
manipulation of me on the bed –
nurses change my position every hour.
The open bedsores suppurate and stink . . .
I am abusive to a social worker.

We, trained Caregivers, can identify
symptoms like this – he is withdrawn and craves
attentive sympathy. Each afternoon
I persist – my ability to bear
his poor responses helps him to contain
his desperation. So there is much comfort.

*   *   *

When I was a boy and read that section at the end of Book V where shipwrecked Laertides crawls under two close-growing olives, one wild one cultivated, exhausted and finds shelter, I was deeply and permanently influenced. Since then the idea of such a comforting and comfortable solitary and impregnable bower has been inseparable for me from the concept of profound sweet sleep – and more . . . Almost every night since that time, except when drunken or erotic diversion has rendered such conceit impracticable, I have snuggled into the warm bedlinen metamorphosing it to dry Sabaean insulating leaves, blanding approaching oblivion.

* * *

[He breaks down and sobs embarrassingly.] The helpless things people scream out so childishly helplessly like 'Oh please I don't want to die I don't want to die I don't *want* to die!' Well, I scream them now I DON'T *WANT* TO   OH HELP ME PLEASE I DON'T *WANT* TO DIE I. [Drivel.] Why write it? Why ever wrote any of it? Poetry all weak lies, games. Epicurus, stupid lies, that there is nothing terrible in not living. Just to stay oh living, oh, why can't I? Stupid childish helpless poor little frightened [Pusillanimous drivel.] frail poor me. Us *all*.

* * *

Verse unvindicable; therefore sublate *The Ballad of Tucker's Tale* (It's once he was a welterweight/And mingled with the champs/ But now he isn't fit, they say,/To make arse-holes for tramps – / Kips in the Council's GRIT FOR ROADS/Fibreglass yellow bin/And Tucker's Tale's known from the *Whale*/To the *Canny Colliers Inn* . . .). During the war, Tucker's squad, randy in France, was queuing up to shag a goat. A lance-corp jumped the queue. Everyone complained, but, while the offender was on the job, his head split suddenly apart leaking grey and crimson. Sniper. Vita brevis; ars ditto.

* * *

Twenty of them. Should be sufficient. Comforting rattle from the brown plastic bottle. Twist of cotton wool. Label typed ONLY AS DIRECTED. Wrapped in linen in the rucksack: the decanter engraved with my initials, the eighteenth-century twist-stemmed glass, the last bottle of 1894 Bual. Yapsel Bank, Hanging Brink, Ashes Hollow, Grindle Nills, Long Synalds. A good enough place to go stiff in. Quite unattended now, on hills where once my sweet wife, my dear daughter . . . (enough of that shite). Oakleymill Waterfall. Skewered by evening sun. Fat, buttery fumosity of amber decanted Madeira. Sour chalkiness of the twentieth pillule.

* * *

I used to pepper my poetics with sophisticated allusions to *dear* Opera and *divine* Art (one was constantly reminded of A. du C. Dubreuil's libretto for Piccinni's *Iphigenia in Tauris*; one was constantly reminded of Niccolò di Bartolomeo da Foggia's bust of a crowned woman, doubtless an allegory of the Church, from the pulpit of Ravello cathedral, ca. 1272) but suddenly these are hopelessly inadequate. Where is the European cultural significance of tubes stuck up the nose, into the veins, up the arse? A tube is stuck up my prick, and a bladder carcinoma diagnosed. One does *not* recall Piccinni.

* * *

My husband never once entertained the notion of transcendentalism. He regarded it as an arrogant ('arrogant humility' is a phrase he used of Buddhism, Christianity &c.), Quaternary, Hominid invention for crudely pacifying the purely physiological characteristic of Hominid cephalic capacity. He viewed the concept of theism as cowardly, conceited, unimaginative and, necessarily, at the *earliest* merely Pliocene. (His period was Precambrian, before god.)

His irascibility increased towards the end . . .

[Missionaries visited him clutching 'Good News' bibles.] You are importunate. Return to your corrugated-iron chapels and crave forgiveness of your wretched deity for disturbing the lucubrations of a bad hat.

* * *

It is a most terrible *bore*
to haemorrhage, spewing-up gore,
and, bubbling for breath,
be blood-drowned to death.
Je *ne* voudrais *pas* être mort.

You find the Limerick inapposite? Care for a cutely-adapted Adonic?

Afer he spewed-up
he was unconscious
till about tea-time,
when he woke up, then
vomited once more
(blood and fish-smelling
purplish matter).
Then he said 'Darling,
please do not leave me,
I think I'm – 'nothing
else. He slumped heavy,
staining my clothing
puce and burnt-umber
(drying black later).
He was my husband –
we had been married
25 good years.

* * *

In ornithological days, at the observatory, we used, not infre-
quently, to discover moribund specimens. They seemed always
to have grovelled into some niche to quietly get on with it – the
stance would so often be trembling on a single weak leg, the lids
half-closed, the grey nictitating membrane half-drawn across the,
by then, dull bead. Several species, on dissection, revealed
carcinomatic infestation.

The use of narcotics, dehydration and breathing through the
mouth have led to his mouth becoming troublesome. We prepare,
in our pharmacy, an artificial saliva containing methyl-cellulose
and glycerin which eases thirst and dry mouth.

* * *

[His wife and daughter tend him at home, bewildered by this
revelation of his, of *all*, frailty. Special Laundry Services deal with
his sheets and blankets – the soiling too foul for acceptance by
normal laundries. The ambulance's arrival would be as the
tumbrel's.]

Briskly efficiently deftly my daughter enters at midnight,
eases me onto my side, changes the oxygen flask.

Even formed properly, no elegiac distich can fall with
quite this sospirity: breath – out of a black mask exhaled.

None of it matters except at a purely personal level:
pain, not oblivion, hurts; as with me, so with all quarks.

* * *

The specialist's hands, extremely large, buff-coloured, gently manipulate my emaciated wrist, two slender bones and a knot of turquoise vein. Huge tawny thumb and forefinger tighten on a frail pulse.

It was a good ferret and almost immediately there was a rabbit in the net. The man I was with (a gyppo-looking type whose company I cultivated as a child but whose name evades me now) removed it from the nylon mesh. His hands were huge and tawny and took up the rabbit, smoothing its ruffled fur, and with soothing fondness, with infinite gentleness, affectionately snapped its neck.

* * *

'His questions were probably mere pleas for reassurance. I did not tell him. I seldom tell them. Some of my colleagues disagree; many are of the same opinion as myself. According to Oken ("What to tell cancer patients", *Journal of the American Medical Association*, 1961, *175*, p 1120), about 80% of us rarely, if ever, tell them.'

According to Gilbertsen and Wangensteen ('Should the doctor tell the patient the disease is cancer?', in *The Physician and the Total Care of the Cancer Patient*, American Cancer Society, New York, 1961), about 80% of patients say they would like to be told.

* * *

His irascibility increased towards the end . . .

I am told that I was rude to a folk-singer who 'writes his own material' (of the You'll-Always-Be-On-My-Mind-Girl/Nuclear-Holocaust-Is-An-Awful-Shame School). He had, at his own considerable expense, caused a record of his ghastly outpourings to be manufactured. He solicited me to buy one. I declined. 'Why?' 'Because I believe you to be devoid of talent, mawkish and platitudinous.' (Sniffily) 'I'm not going to stay here and be insulted.' He went. It was as if one had flicked a smut from one's lapel.

* * *

'Quite the most maudlin man I've ever met
told me this in the lounge of the *Colliers*:
"It's many years ago now but, oh God!,
I can still feel her hand rubbing my tool
as she drove slowly down the pleached-hedged lane.
She stopped the car, licked her lips, moaned, and kissed me –

Christ!, slurping tongues like squirming warm oiled slugs –
and said 'God!, I could eat you' and unzipped
my washed-out Levi's, peeled them apart and guzzled.
I'll never see her again – I've got bowel cancer."'
Run them together, set as justified prose
the inadequately blank pentameters.

* * *

68

Now for a bit of a trip down Memory Lane. Spring breakfast, bluebells on sun-dappled gingham. A blue-hooped jug of cream, bronzed toast, Frank Cooper's. Smoked aromatic crepitating rashers. FREE!!! IN EACH PACK OF *BRAN-BREK* – A PLASTIG BUG!!! I am served a dusty handful, read the packet. *Medical Scientists are in agreement. We all need fibre, and bran is full of fibre. BRAN-BREK is full of bran, so eat BRAN-BREK. Doctors say fibreless diets cause bowel cancer. Don't take the risk – get into the BRAN-BREK habit.* What was then fear has become shitless terror.

* * *

Have you ever been in one of them? They really are depressing. Anyway, we were visiting someone – actually, the husband's mother it was, and the kid was with us so it all rather comes home to you that in a few years that'll be *you* in that bed and the kid, grown up, with *its* kid, visiting *you* . . . Anyway, in the next bed was this, you can only call it 'thing', – no bedclothes, just an official nightdress thing – and while we were telling lies to *our* one, *it* started up a sort of whining gurgling wheezing noise. [**To be continued.**]

* * *

[**Contd.**] I tried to crack on I hadn't noticed anything, but it kept on and on and I saw it was trying to attract my attention so I couldn't do anything but try to savvy what it was on about. It couldn't move, except sort of rock its head and flap one arm against its side. And all the time that queer noise. Its mouth wouldn't close and whenever it made that noise 'Waahg waahgrrglz' spittle with streaks of red dribbled out. It turned out that it wanted the screens pulled round it, and *I* had to do it. *Uuuugh!*

* * *

I seen him once before, before – you know. I was fetching a white Welsh, 12 hands, down Grindle Nills. Between Grindle Hollow and Oakleymill there was him and his Mrs and nipper. Picnicking, they was, wine cooling in the brook. He gawped at the nag's pricked ears, large eye, dished profile, withers, mane, poll, forelock, muzzle, chin, cheek, shoulder, chest, forearm, knee, cannon, pastern, chestnut, brisket, elbow, belly, stifle, gaskin, coronet, wall of hoof, heel, fetlock, hock, thigh, buttock, dock, croup, loins, back. He knew who I was alright. 'That's a pale one ye have there, Mr Tucker' he said.

* * *

At the end of the Cambrian, an estimated 52% of faunal families became extinct. At the end of the Devonian, 30%. At the end of the Permian, 50%. At the end of the Triassic, 35%. At the end of the Cretacious, 26%. Last night I had to get up frequently and stagger to the bathroom at the end of the ward. Pain unendurable. Rocked back and forth on lavatory seat, groaning. At the end of the Holocene (fashionable Tropical Rain Forest reduction, fashionable Nuclear Holocaust) the percentage of faunal family extinction is likely to at least compare with Cambrian figures.

* * *

[He writes] *Dear* [names of his wife and child which I render 'A' and 'B' for reasons of delicacy], *I recall our Callow Hollow alfresco. Our tiny child bathing in Oakleymill Waterfall pool. A gorse sprig suspended in an eddy. We were at the best of our lives. Such happiness never recurs. Never. Golden bright little flower, sharp thorns. Spätlese cooling in the gelid spring. Later, the gipsy with that pale gelding. I will remember these things until the day I die.* [Which is the day after tomorrow. He signs his name which I render 'C' for reasons of delicacy.]

* * *

'Retention can give rise to undue pain;/ incontinence, conversely, causes shame/and a degree of inconvenience./ Colostomies, short-circuiting the bowel/to open on the frontal abdomen,/can cause distress at first, but nothing like/the anguish that the blockage, not relieved,/would cause. Soon after surgery, it seems,/ some soiling from the new colostomy/is unavoidable – patients become/aware that they can get unclean and smell . . .'

Terminal verse. Rain-pits 700000000 years old in Precambrian rock: a species evolved 696000000 years after that: a handful of stresses and punctuation: ars only as long as vita: pentameters, like colons, inadequate.

*   *   *

100 days after diagnosis, I ingest soporifics. I compose octave and first line of sestet concerning my cadaver.

> The vagrant Tucker found it, partly rotted,
> Eyes gouged by corvids, puffed blue meat, wet, stinking,
> Blown lips serrated (nibbled as if pinking-
> Shears had been at them), maggoty nose besnotted.
> From its arse pocket he took five green-spotted
> (With penicillia) £5 notes – thinking,
> Quite rightly, they'd be better used for drinking
> Bass in *The Whale* than festering, rank, clotted
>
> In [something something something] Ashes Hollow

Why? snot, gore, filth, suppuration of the arse-gut – for these *no* metric is vindicable.

*   *   *

A regular at the *Colliers* was Head of Art at the local Poly (phoney smoothie, used to take snuff). Mort bought some Itchy Powder from the *Wizard's Den* Joke Shop and one evening, when the Art bloke offered the old silver snuff-box round the bar, our hero slipped the irritant in (looked just like snuff) and handed back the antique. The offensive educationalist took no more stimulant until, on the motorway, driving back home, he indulged, and, in the paroxysm of sneezing that ensued, collided with an oncoming articulated lorry hauling meat-and-bone-meal and was killed instantly.

* * *

In the Borough Library the medical dictionaries are mostly used by unfortunates looking up their maladies. The Cs are particularly well-thumbed. **CARCINAEMIA CARCINECTOMY CARCINELCOSIS CARCINOGEN CARCINOGENESIS CARCINOGENIC CARCINOGENICITY CARCINOID CARCINOLOGY CARCINOLYSIN CARCINOLYSIS CARCINOLYTIC CARCINOMATOID CARCINOMATO-PHOBIA CARCINOMATOSIS CARCINOMATOUS CAR-CINOMECTOMY CARCINOMELCOSIS CARCINO-PHILIA CARCINOPHILIC CARCINOPHOBIA CARCI-NOSARCOMA CARCINOSECTOMY CARCINOSIS CAR-CINOSTATIC CARCINOUS.** I am researching **C. ventriculi**; the woman who has just relinquished Stedman's has marked faintly in pencil **C. of uterine cervix**. We are beyond verse here. No one wants to write 'On Last Looking Into Stedman's Carcinoma'. Nevertheless, I have invented the 13-line sonnet for unlucky people (100 words, inc. title) . . .

* * *

TALKING SHOP

The three sterilizations went OK,
except for the advanced C. uterine cervix
(just my damned luck to find that) – anyway,
apart from that it all went normally.
The one in Number 2 was staggered when
I said 'We found your coil, by the way –
worked its way through the womb into the space
between the womb and stomach.' Number 3
(non compos mentis, got eight kids already)
asked me when 'it' would be alright again.
I said 'If you endeavour to avoid
sexual intercourse for about two nights . . .'
She said 'He won't wait. He *will* have his rights.'

* * *

His irascibility increased towards the end . . .

    The sham the twee and the precious/phoney-rustic ignor-ant/wield their sugary Biros/down in the safe Sticks/ensconced in the done-up Old Wheelwright's./Poetical mawkish duff gen/ where a buzzard is 'noble' and lands/in a tree (surprise, surprise!)/to corroborate some trite tenet/cum badly-observed Nature Note./ Their fauna is furry or feathery/people like you and me,/cute or nasty – a raptor/becomes a Belfast terrorist./ Bull-shit bull-shit bull-shit/of the Plashy Fen School./Peterson, Mountfort & Hollom/write more sense than you/bloody carpetbaggers.

*   *   *

According to Parkes ('Bereavement and mental illness', *British Journal of Medical Psychology*, 1965, *38*, p 1), 8% of seriously distressed bereaved people questioned expressed anger towards the dead person.

'She didn't seem particularly distraught. We were just with her at the ceremony. Suddenly she just seemed to ignore us all. "Why have you left me, why have you gone away? Why have you left me, why have you gone away? Why have you left me, why have you gone away? Why have you left me, why have you gone away?" She yelled and yelled as it went into the furnace.'

*   *   *

Muse! Sing *Phylloscopus trochiloides!*/I know it is a strange thing to recall/out of a rag-bag of experience/(rather than, say, rude goings-on with girls/or that first fright of Death – lost in thick fog/ and with the tide coming in rapidly/over the mud-flats in the river mouth . . .),/but, more than early childhood or first dick,/ this vagrant (which I mist-netted in youth)/incongruously glad-dens my last thoughts/(and, more incongruous still, in quator-zain)./The wing formula confirmed that it was Greenish/(rather than Arctic) Warbler – longer first/and shorter second primary, of course.

*　*　*

We went to picnic up Calo Holow to have a picnic to a wortofall and a pool the pool was very deep. I neely fell into the pool. it was very suney We had cold chicin. Daddy and Mummy lay in the gras by the streem and I played round about and had oranj juse then Mummy and daddy had some wine that was cooling in the streem. Here is a powim of it

> When I went up Calo Hill
> I took some orang I did not spill.
>
> we saw a pale grey poniy
> Daddy fel asleep by the streem

*　*　*

It's bad for us as well, you know, looking after them. Can you take any more? I can't. I'm ready to give up. What's the use? All our patients die eventually. They should do six things for their 'Death Work': (1) become aware of their impending death, (2) balance hope and fear throughout the crisis, (3) *reverse* physical survival instincts, (4) relinquish independence, (5) detach themselves from former experiences and (6) prepare 'spiritually' for death. They go through six emotional states (outlined by Kübler-Ross): (1) Denial, (2) Isolation, (3) Anger, (4) Bargaining, (5) Depression, (6) Acceptance. All, eventually. All.

* * *

These are the sorts of things they say, through six emotional states (outlined by Kübler-Ross), sad, self-deceiving till the last ones: 'It's just one of those things' 'I shall be out of here soon' 'I'm getting better' 'I'm feeling fine' 'It's not so bad' 'I just need a good tonic' 'Be back at work before you can say "Jack Robinson"' 'My pneumonia's worse than my cancer'. Can you take any more? I can't. I'm ready to give up. What's the use? All our patients die eventually. Anyway, those are the things they first say, DENIAL. Next comes ISOLATION:

* * *

'You don't know how it feels' 'You can't know how it feels' 'No one understands' 'They don't tell you anything' 'I try to guess what's going on' 'On your morning rounds you seem too busy to talk' 'No one seems to realize how vital my supply of oxygen is' 'I try to hide my feelings so that the family's not too distressed' 'Don't like being on my own' 'I don't like being left alone'. Those who we have not told start to sense it – the way the nurses look at them, the way we see less and less of them . . .

* * *

Next comes ANGER: 'Why *me*?' 'They don't care' 'It's *my* body – they treat you like a child of 3' 'The food's lousy' 'The Quack's no good' 'A God of Love – huh!' 'The nurses is lazy' 'Why don't this happen to the scroungers and layabouts?' 'Doctor's a fool if he thinks this treatment will work'. Next comes BARGAINING: 'If only I could be home for the daughter's wedding, I'd not care after that' 'If only I could go without pain, I wouldn't mind so much' 'If only God would spare me to do His work a little longer, wouldn't mind then'.

* * *

Can you take any more? I can't. I'm ready to give up. What's the use? All our patients die eventually. By now they can no longer depend on their bodies doing what, before they got ill, they thought they would do in such an eventuality – neither suicide, nor smart philosophizing. They can not conceive beforehand what it will be like. Dying nobly? My sweet arse hole. One of them wrote verse. Verse! Write verse about this: a Left Inguinal Colostomy. Shit, blood, puke and a body no longer dependable, metastases, dyspnoea . . . I shut my eyes but weep under the lids.

* * *

The fifth emotional state (outlined by Kübler-Ross) is that of DEPRESSION: 'What chance have I got?' 'Not long now' 'What's the use?' 'This cancer is the end of everything' 'I'm not going to get better' 'I'm so useless now'. Last comes ACCEPT-ANCE: 'Thank you for all you've done' 'Dying will be a relief' 'I see things differently now' 'The wife will be so terribly lost and lonely'. These are the sorts of things they say through the six emotional states (outlined by Kübler-Ross), sad, self-deceiving till the last ones. It's bad for us as well, you know.

* * *

I ndian doctor examines N ewly performed colotomy (is appalled).	3

T erminal case, brought into H ere last night, won't E ver return to Azalea Terrace.	2

S mall frightened old woman, A fter anaesthetic, has dim M emory of fainting in chip-shop (won't E ver get out of here).	1

V ery smooth-looking E xecutive-type in R oad accident; surgeons T ry to revive him, fail; I n collison with lorry C arrying meat-and-bone-meal. A n elderly lady, supposed suicidal, L oudly denies taking barbiturates.	G

C oke is shovelled O nto the furnace by a L oathsome old stoker who now U nfolds the Sports Page, M arks with an X some N ag for the next Meeting.	B

Mort or *Char* (this latter pronounced 'chair' or 'care' in their infernal accents, though, presumably, merely short for Charlie) possesses many katabolic anecdotes. His erstwhile leman bestowed finger-nail and teeth impressions on the mantelpiece as her distemper flourished and the burden of pain induced gripping and biting the mahogany often for hours together in the full excruciating anguish of the paroxysm. The huge firm 18-year-old malleable boobs she had let him enjoy were defiled at 42 by surgeon's scalpel and radium treatment. This, rendered into catalectic tetrameters, might do for the *TLS* or other reputable literary periodical.

* * *

What were bronzed on Margate sands,
flopped about by trembling hands,
malleable, conical,
have become ironical.
What was cupped in palm and thumb
seres now under radium.
What was kneaded like warm dough
is where, now, malign cells grow.
What was fondled in a car
through white silk-smooth slippery bra
(Marks & Spencer, 38)
was plump cancer inchoate.

Truncation (catalexis): 'frequent in trochaic verse, where the line of complete trochaic feet tends to create monotony. The following trochaic lines exhibit t.: "Simple maiden, void of art,/ Babbling out the very heart" . . .' – *Princeton Encyclopedia of Poetry and Poetics* (ed. Preminger).

* * *

He speaks to me and doodles the disorder's initial letter with green Biro in his desk-diary. Croissant? Banana? Sickle blade? He is frightened of what I will ask. Some of them will not tell you, nor prescribe what you really need. Perhaps an accumulation from a bogus insomnia claim, then, after the magnum of '61 *Cheval Blanc*, end with the 19th century Bual before taking them. Stylish finish, with the fine initialled decanter. Green discharge smothers the hideous curve, enormous now, and a suppurating colon punctuates it. I can almost scent the *Cheval Blanc* as I think of it.

*   *   *

when she first found it feel this she said oh god it can't be can it lump probably nothing he said better just x-ray be on safe side swarming teeming oh god if could turn back calendar only a few pages she went bald radium god pain bald horrible years ago on the Med when she god they were magnificent huge golden tanned god bald like a skull hugest on the beach

[Cold truncating surgeon's blade
razes what was St Tropezed.

Tomorrow she will occupy the 2nd floor Infirmary bed where now a patient from Azalea Terrace is expiring.]

*   *   *

'The husband was driving. The wife, aged 23, was in the back seat. They were on the motorway. She had just been discharged from a mental institution. Without comment she took 20 barbiturates. Suddenly the young man became aware that she was comatose on the sheepskin cover. He observed the empty brown plastic phial. In panic he screeched into a Services Area and – ' 'Why had she tried to, you know?' 'Terrible fear of getting cancer, no reason to suspect it, just kept thinking she would.' (Great unvindicable idea: a 17-liner, 100-word, pentameter acrostic, first letters forming *CARCINOMATOPHOBIA*.) 'Continue.'

*　*　*

'He carried her into the Ladies' Lavatory intending to make her puke up the offending drug. She could not be made to vomit. An elderly lady, unable to enter the lavatory because it was thus occupied, sat on a chair outside the cubicle. Frenzied, the young husband raced to telephone for an ambulance, leaving his spouse unconscious in the toilet. He dialled 999 on the Cafeteria phone. The Cafeteria Manageress forced him to consume three cups of hot sweet tea. Meanwhile, ambulancemen arrived, accused the seated elderly lady of ingesting barbiturates, and, despite her protestations, bore her away by stretcher.'

*　*　*

*C*onstantly anticipating cancer/(*A*bdominal, lung, throat, breast, uterus,/*R*ectum, 'malevolent' or 'benign'), she went/*C*rackers and was soon certifiable./*I*nside, the loopiest of all was the/*N*ut-doctor who prescribed barbiturates/'*O*nly as soporifics – one per night'./*M*onths passed, and she accumulated 20./*A*t length she was discharged. Her husband called/*T*o chauffeur her. 'Apparently depressed/*O*r meditative, otherwise OK,/*P*erhaps a change of scene? . . .' Motoring back,/*H*opelessly fraught, she polished off the lot./*O*verdose verdict brought by coroner . . . /*B*loody fool ambulance-wallahs kidnapped some/*I*dle bystander (who they thought looked ill)/*A*nd left the suicide slumped in the bogs.

* * *

Ubi sunt the blue-green algae of yesteryear that by photosynthesis first oxygenated the atmosphere? In the black cherts of the Bulawayan Limestone Group dated at about three thousand one hundred million years old, in the stromatolitic sediments first noted by Macgregor, later corroborated by Schopf et al; that is where. *Ubi sunt* the good old rain-pits and ripple-marks so transiently formed about six hundred million years ago? Buried in the Late Precambrian Longmyndian matrices of this valley where I myself . . . What is 40 years here or there on the chronostratigraph? (They don't make them like that anymore.)

* * *

When I worked with Schopf, on the Bulawayan stromatolites, I took twelve specimens of the limestone, each having a maximum dimension of 15 cm and exhibiting one or more areas of iron-stained, crescentic laminations of weathered surfaces. The best of these exhibited seven areas of lamination on the external surfaces and I gently broke it along the planes of weakness perpendicular to the laminations, exposing five additional laminated areas. I photographed the broken fragments and prepared a plaster cast of each. Those laminates were 3100000000 years old; I am dying (Carcinoma ventriculi) but the Holocene is of scant importance.

* * *

Ubi sunt J. William Schopf, Dorothy Z. Oehler, Robert J. Horodyski and Keith A. Kvenvolden, whose 'Biogenicity and Significance of the Oldest Known Stromatolites' (Journal of Paleontology, V. 45, No. 3, p. 477–485) so inspired us? They are now one with the cold stromatolitic limestone and laminated carbonaceous cherts of the Huntsman Limestone Quarries near Turk Mine, 55 km north-north-east of Bulawayo; that is where. *Ubi sunt* God? and pusillanimous Nietzsche (who merely substituted Übermenschen)? Sedimented. *Ubi sunt* Übermenschen? and the Master of the 100 100-Word Units? Sedimented, sedimented. (They don't make them like that anymore.)

* * *

'They are angry with their own failing bodies . . . also apt to criticize and blame others . . . One such aggrieved . . . greatly troubled the nurses and doctors who cared for her . . . Often young nurses would leave her bedside to shed a few tears because their attempts to help her had been met by contemptuous dismissal . . . accusing those who were treating her of apathy inefficiency and callousness . . . a way of expressing her disappointment and bitterness . . . for herself and the life that seemed unfulfilled . . .' – John Hinton, *Dying*, (Penguin, 1967).

His irascibility increased towards the end . . .

'Piss off, Sky Pilot', I whisper in the Padre's ear.

*   *   *

Sky cerulean. Sheep-cropped moist short sprung bright green turf where I lie, face up, my head on a stone at the brook edge. Upstream a metre and downstream a metre, trickling sound registers in each ear, an alto tinkling, a basso gurgling, the upper notes resembling skylark song, the lower resembling bathwater unplugged, concurrently continuously varying. My bare arms warm in bright sun. My husband beside me, touches. Suddenly our young daughter hugs me, hugs me again. Gewürztraminer rocks in the cool current. Cold roasted partridges in a white linen towel. Late Autumn, but, something irrevocably pleasant has occurred.   lovely

*   *   *

My ward, 1A, was called Harley Ward (after the famous street, I assume). On arrival I was led into a tiny office to fill in forms which included questions like 'Have you been living in the UK for more than 12 months?' and 'Have your mother and father been living in the UK for more than 12 months?' Then I was labelled: a plastic strap was snapped round my wrist and inside its waterproof sheath was my name and number and what I was in for – colotomy. This perhaps reduces the likelihood of some innocent part being removed by mistake.

* * *

(Not just me, but all of us in the same vertical column. I pass the same hopeless pyjamad cases in ghastly contraptions daily. In the snot-green corridors daily the covered trolleys are shunted. Daily the meat-waggons swing through the gates braying, pulsing blue light, their burdens already history scraped off the Tarmac. Daily and nightly the trolleys the trolleys the trolleys jingle like gently shaken tambourines as they hasten with cargoes of shiny stainless-steel kidney-shaped bowls and glinting clamps, needles and blades and forceps, acres of soft white lint to one or another and finally all.)

* * *

Then I was led to my bed and shown my locker. I was to undress, stow away my clothes and lie down. A nurse curtained me off from the others. She recorded my temperature and pulse, took my blood pressure and shaved me with an old razor across the stomach from the navel down, removing about an inch of pubic hair. Then I produced a urine sample in a bed pan. After that there was nothing to do until the anaesthetist was due to see me at 5 pm. I produced my *Times* which was stolen by a marauding nurse.

*   *   *

The doctor had told me but not him. One evening he was struggling with a pile of papers – administrative stuff, to do with the conference on Early Precambrian Stromatolite Morphology and Taxonomy – when he slumped into his seat, exhausted by the simple exertion. I touched his arm and said (I hear my voice and its slight echo from the sparsely furnished study as if it is played back to me on tape) 'Oh my darling, you should not trouble with anything unessential; you see, you are dying.' He simply replied 'I understand' and replaced the documents in the mahogany bureau.

*   *   *

Radio-2 blared over a loudspeaker system. There was a radio with earphones behind my bed, so I tried to tune in to something else. There was a dial which read RADIO-1 RADIO-2 RADIO-3 RADIO-4. I clicked the indicator around the dial through three-hundred-and-sixty degrees. Radio-2 was vigorously transmitted at every calibration on the instrument. A trolley was driven at me by a gentleman with dirty fingernails. This vehicle supported a large urn of grey tea and a material bearing the legend BRAN SPONGE, BY THE MAKERS OF BRAN-BREK. I declined.

* * *

(Not just me, but out there in the Pedestrianized Precincts. The filth gathers beyond clearance or control. In gales the crisp yellow newspapers soar above the high-rises and out to sea or lodge in electric wires or pile up against shop doors. New desolate sounds of Coke cans discarded tinkling rolling in windy streets over greasy flags, and cables slapped clacking against tin masts of yachts in deserted lidos. In Department Stores staff outnumber customers now. The Cosmetics assistants, painted like Archie Andrews, look frightened at scant trade. In Furnishings, Glassware, Heel Bar, Carpeting . . . something irrevocably dying is happening.)

* * *

The anaesthetist arrived, tampered with my heart and lungs, felt all round the ribs and implored me to breathe deeply while he listened. My blood pressure was up. He seemed desirous I should sleep and prescribed a soporific. I should be given a pre-med injection in the thigh about 2 pm on Tuesday and about 3 pm be taken into the Recovery Room and injected in the back of the hand to 'knock me out completely'. He'd 'bring me round' again and I'd be trundled back to bed. Incongruously, he inspected my fingernails. No doubt he found them charming.

* * *

Newsflash, their women writhe unconsolable in the dirt of Ulster and the Holy Land. They are not actresses; that is how they really feel. How I feel also, my cancerous husband. Newsflash after newsflash, their women writhe unconsolable in the dirt of Ulster and the Holy Land. They are not actresses; that is how they really feel. How I feel also, my cancerous husband. Newsflash after newsflash after stinking newsflash, their women writhe unconsolable in the dirt of Ulster and the Holy Land. They are not actresses; that is how they really feel. How I feel also, my cancerous husband.

* * *

I was fed Health Authority Chicken Supreme and semolina and jam and made to watch television where a woman turned into a spider during the full-moon, hunted respectable citizens, injected them with poison, swathed them in web cocoons and carried them off to her Transylvanian silo. I was given Ovaltine and sleeping-draught and endured insomnia all night. On Tuesday I was given tea at 6 am. 'Have you "performed"?' 'What do you mean?' I was given a suppository and told to keep it in for 20 minutes. I got cramp up the arse and shat after 5 minutes.

* * *

(Not just me, but the public clocks in the cities are fucked-up – / the Building Society one, the one on the Bank,/the one on the Town Hall, the one at the Station, all stopped/at a hopeless time and, whereas when I was a child/they were constants to be relied on, now the resources/and requisite knowledge to fix them are gone. And this isn't/some crusty superannuated old Colonel/ lamenting, saying 'Of course, it was all fields then . . .',/but me, as my cardio-whatsit ticks limply, observing/the clocks all knackered, whereas they used not to be.)

* * *

I have invented
a brand new kind of sonnet
where the octave is
a tanka plus a haiku
and the sestet two haikus.
But is there, today,
one ghastly experience
that vindicates verse?

Outside the chip-shop
an ambulance's blue light
throbs at heartbeat rate.
Someone has dropped dead;
tidily weighed syllables
drip from the draped stiff.

Why *verse*? At **PRIDE OF PLAICE,** the chippy opposite the
Leisure Centre, a horrible old human is slouched with its head
cradled in the alarmed proprietor's arms. Nearby a beggar swigs
White Horse, grey abrasive palm like a parched tongue anticipating small coin.

*   *   *

Char helped the Undertaker once. The passenger had lived alone in a cottage with a couple of dogs. It sat rigid in an armchair, sap-green translucent glaze over the cheekbones. Char smoothed the back of his finger gently over the brow (the skin was unpliable, cool, waxen) then leered, and between thumb and grimy palm grasped the yellow lardy chin and shook it with hatred. The grey tongue lolled. One of the dogs, a trembling whippet, mounted the cadaver's bare knee, ejaculating after several minutes' rut. Char pocketed £25 from the mantelpiece, lowered the stiff into its fibreglass vessel.

* * *

Breakfast at 8 am was toast and tea. This was to be my last food for 24 hours. At 11 am I had a Savlon bath. I was given a sachet of concentrated disinfectant to put in the water and told to immerse to the ears and wash the face in it. I was put in surgical robes of crisp white linen and a gauze cap and returned to bed. I waited thus absurdly for the anaesthetist. Radio-2 was statutory. The first injection was 'in the bottom to gently relax you'. I scrutinized the ceiling for signs of change.

* * *

When I worked with Schopf on the Huntsman Quarry stromatolites, we concluded that the Bulawayan deposit could be interpreted as placing a minimum age (ca 3100000000 yrs) on the origin of cyanophycean algae, of the filamentous habit, and of integrated biological communities of procaryotic micro-organisms presumably including producers (blue-green algae), reducers (aerobic and anaerobic bacteria) and consumers (bacteria, predatory by absorption). This interpretation was supported by the occurrence of filamentous and unicellular alga-like and bacterium-like microfossils in other Early Precambrian sediments. I am dying (Carcinoma ventriculi) but what is 40 years here or there on the chronostratigraph?

* * *

Everything became pellucid. I seemed on the brink of some revelation or original idea. Then I ceased to focus and my eye-lids felt heavy. I think I dozed because the time went very quickly. A Romany-looking stretcher-bearer shuttled to and fro. I couldn't establish what he did with his poles. The stretchers were canvas. A trolley would come in. He inserted his poles. A patient was eased into bed. The poles were removed. I could not see what he did with the poles. I became irascible. I wanted to demand testily of him 'Account for your poles, sir!'.

* * *

I should have started my sabbatical
but now it is impossible. Six weeks
ago they took the part-time employee,
hired to replace me, into hospital,
opened him up and said he had three months
before he pegged out – cancerous guts. They fetched
some out, but found too much inside.

                                        He keeps
a sort of journal, so they say, in which
he chronicles his death in the 3rd Person,
partly in prose, part verse, peculiar, hey?
He's only young-ish too. So that's the end
of my sabbatical – I'm pretty miffed
(nor, I suppose, is he too chuffed about it).

                        *   *   *

I helped myself onto the stretcher. I was wheeled through the double doors into a bathroom-green room. The anaesthetist slapped my hand to raise a vein. 'You'll feel a small prick and a little scratch. There. Now it should be beginning to take effect.' I tried to say yes but said yuriuree. 'You may be feeling a cold sensation.' Yurayuaress. A masked nurse in green said 'Can you see me? Can you focus on my face?' I tried to say yes but couldn't. I tried to say wind but said wiznera ah. She raised my head and I farted.

* * *

No verse is|adequate.‖Most of us|in this ward
will not get|out again.‖This poor sod|next to me
will be dead|in a month.‖He is young,|has not been
married long,|is afraid‖(so am I,|so am I).
When his wife|visits him‖(every day,|every day)
he takes hold|of her sleeve,‖clutches her|savagely
screaming 'Please,|get me well!‖Dear sweet God,|make me well!'
Quasi sham|tétramètre,‖sub Corneille,|sub Racine,
is too grand,|is too weak,‖for this slow|tragedy,
screaming 'Please,|get me well!‖Dear sweet God,|make me well!'

* * *

Wheeled back to bed. I try to lift my arms. Cannot. The Romany performs with his mysterious poles. I am told to get some sleep. Staff Nurse calls the stretcher-blankets 'cuddlies'. Throat rusk-dry. I am uncomfortable but unable to turn onto my side. Eventually I heave myself onto my side . . . At an unknown time tea is brought. I feel sick. They wash my face and hands. The rubber under the sheets makes me sweat. BRAN-BREK is proffered. The surgeon who performed it appears. A pleasant, worried Sikh. He is afraid of what I am going to ask.

* * *

(Not just me, but also, out there, the cities whose shit/surges into the sea in tsunamis,/and Shopping Precincts whose shit of canines and rolling/Coke tins and paper and fag-ends and polystyrene/chip-trays and plastic chip-forks rattle in bleak winds,/and those who wash least, breed most, to all of us, all,/a shoddy incontrovertible burial in shit./

This isn't some crusty Colonel (retired) lamenting/'Of course it was all fields then, you see, in those days . . .',/but me, me, suppurating to death,/not just on my own but with us all, with us all.)

* * *

Ubi sunt Chaloner ALABASTER, Guido BACH, William CADGE, William Otto Adolph Julius DANCKWERTS, His Excellency Dr Johannes Friedrich August von ESMARCH, His Honour Judge William Wynne FFOULKES, Sydney GRUNDY, Henry HOOK, Eugene Clutterbuck IMPEY, James JOICEY, Nesbitt KIRCHHOFFER, Chih Chen LO FENG-LUH, Budgett MEAKIN, Alfred Trubner NUTT, John Orlando Hercules Norman OLIVER, Mrs PUDDICOMBE, Harry QUILTER, Rt. Hon. Sir Horace RUMBOLD, John SPROT, Gaspard le Marchant TUPPER, Emanual Maguire UNDERDOWN, Thomas Henry Bourke VADE-WALPOLE, Edward Montagu Granville Montagu Stuart Wortley Mackenzie WHARN-CLIFFE, His Honour Judge Lawford YATE-LEE, Guiseppe ZANARDELLI? (In *Who Was Who 1897–1915*, that's where.)

* * *

Some of us benefit from a self-shielding shunning of awful
thoughts about dying and, worse, physical pain at the end.

Nevertheless we are conscious of being falsely deluding,
when we say jauntily 'Oh! I shall be out of here soon!'

Adequate realization of what is truly awaiting
does not prevent us from this: never admitting we *know*.

Even though sometimes I talk about this abdominal cancer,
my mental ease demands lies, comfort of make-believe games –

such as this one that I play now in distich, almost pretending
verse has validity. No. Verse is fuck-all use here, now.

* * *

The meat-waggon comes for another unfortunate. Borne out of Azalea Terrace, the disgusting old victim looks glum, stunned, stupid, no longer working properly. There is bright pink spit dribbling onto the clean black sleeve of an ambulance man who holds one end of a stainless steel wheelchair thing and cradles the nasty head. Cold metallic joints lock slickly. A disinfectant whiff. One-way window. Blue pulse. Sitting on a yellow fibreglass road-grit bunker, the Mad Tramp pulls at a whisky bottle (White Horse) and guffaws a perfect pentameter:

Hă há|hă há|hă há|hă há|hă há.

* * *

Evolution (including mass faunal extinction, at the end of the Cambrian, Holocene &c.) is what happens – not what *should*, according to *sapiens* interpretations, happen.

It seems to be the greatest pain I've known in my life. Respiration fails because of it, sweat streams, I think (I *hope*) I'll faint under it. Members of hospital staff are conditioned to pay no heed to (nor administer sufficient analgesics for) such excruciation. I feel mental as well as physical strain and inadequacy.

None of it *matters* (except at a purely personal level). Pain, not oblivion, hurts. As with me, so with all quarks.

* * *

[He breaks down and sobs embarrassingly.] Oh! I shall miss you so. Why has it happened? Why has stuff inside me suddenly gone terribly wrong? I don't think I'm afraid of not *being* anymore but so terribly terribly frightened of not being *with you*. And the child; no more playing catch with that large red-and-blue-spotted plastic ball. Never. Anymore. She called it Mr Spotty. [Mawkish drivel.] I can't be brave tonight. Oh my darling, help me! Look after me! Can't be brave or consoled by philosophy or by po – would willingly never have written anything if *only*

* * *

He had just died and screens surrounded the bed but the porter had not had opportunity to remove the body. I arrived at Visiting Hour when all the nurses were busy and unable to intercept me. I went straight to the screened bed and, employing a funny voice (derived from Donald Duck) which we had developed during our years of marriage for times of particular playfulness, addressed the occupant through the plastic panel thus: 'Howsqush my dearsqush old drake thisqush evening-sqush?'. Visitors at adjacent beds regarded me patronizingly. Then I bobbed my head round the screen and confronted the shroud.

* * *

[He writes] *Darling* [names of wife and daughter] *won't last (too weak) till Visiting Hour. Hope you find this. Last notes. Biro on Kleenex, fitting medium terminal words. Oh! Oh weep for Adonais he is dead. C3: the lowest grade of physical fitness in Military Service. On the filthy window-ledge of this ward a foul cleg in a patina of grease and dust whizzes around and around and. The only way to cross the Acheron is on inflated egos. Sleep after toil, port after stormy seas, Ease after war, death after life does greatly please. Two last Spenserians?* [Pah.]

* * *

Interdenominational claptrap,
from the Infirmary Chaplains, helps a few
cowardly of us bear our deaths. The chap
whom they leucotomized conceives this true:
that his soul is eternal. Such a view,
wholly unsatisfactory for me,
is genuinely good – he won't pull through,
but hopes to die without finality
accepting their dud-specious immortality.

Other poltroons amongst us, though, are scared
not of not *being* any more, but just
of terminal agony, are unprepared
[3ll. of MS. lacking ....
....
....]
Still more of us fear pain *and* being dust,
and for us nothing can (nor god, nor soul,
nor analgesic, nor philosophy) console.

* * *

101

It started with his urinating blood. We looked at it in the lavatory pan and were terrified. He went to morning surgery. He had to go for tests. They found he had a bladder carcinoma, little mushroomy things – we saw a photo. They forced something into him through a tube stuck into his penis hole. After the op they kept the tube in for a long time. It caused him to have a hard-on all the time it was in. He was in pain. He had to have regular check-ups. It seemed clear for ages, but recurred, *massively*.

* * *

[He breaks down and sobs embarrassingly.] I keep thinking *if only*. Oh, help me! And I can't believe it – that I am really going to   It is as if I were just writing about someone else d – just as if it were yet another of the things about those poor *other* people that I write (*used to* write) about. Why am I writing about it? Can't be brave tonight. [Drivel.] Oh, my darling, if only I could stay here not go not go not die! [Drivel.] Oh, I shall miss you so [Drivel.] terribly! terribly! Oh my dear darl [&c.]

* * *

Of course I have read Beecher ('The measurement of pain', *Pharmacological Reviews*, 1957, *9*, p. 59) and know that these opium-derived analgesics exert their principal effect not on the original pain but on the psychological processing of that pain. At first the effect was to allay fear and induce calm, even ecstasy. But my increasing tolerance to large doses and my increasing need for the drug have led them to consider Pennybacker's idea ('Management of intractable pain', *Proceedings of the Royal Society of Medicine*, 1963, *56*, p. 191) of leucotomy, meddling with the thalamus or with the frontal lobe.

* * *

Now I envisage the lachrymose mourning of my wife who loved
                                                            me,
there is the clearing of drawers, folding of vacated clothes.

'Here is the T-shirt and here are the denims he wore in the
                                                        summer,
well, he was then, and robust. Here is the green and red shirt

worn, I remember, as we walked together last year on his
                                                        birthday.
Here are the shoes he last wore – still in the treads of one heel

dry worms of mud and dead bracken remain from that day on
                                                    Long Synalds.'
Empty, amorphous and cold, blue tubes of Levi's. She weeps.

* * *

'They feel worthlessness and emptiness without the deceased. "Now I am nothing." "Feel empty inside." (Loss of self-esteem.) They wish to believe the deceased is not dead. Happy and sad memories of the deceased. Concern for the deceased's missing life-enjoyment. "I am here not deserving to be alive while he is dead, unable to enjoy this lovely day." (Guilt.) "It is a dream; he'll be back tomorrow." (Need to deny the loss.) "I've disposed of his clothing." (Demonstrates *either* ability to relinquish bond to the deceased *or* compulsion to rid themselves of the pain which that clothing evokes.)'

* * *

Here are some of the things you'll need if it takes place at home: bed-care utensil set (inc. denture cup, kidney basin, bed pan &c.), large sheet of plastic, rented wheelchair, box of flexible drinking-straws, one bag disposable bed pads (the incontinent will use considerably more), large size disposable diapers (several boxes), thermometer, one bottle ethyl alcohol, cotton balls, lubricant, commode, a great many spare under-sheets, six wash-cloths.

Each nostril must be cleaned with a twist of tissue or cotton wool. Eyelids should be swabbed with wool swabs and warm normal saline, especially in the morning.

* * *

Since I deal daily with the incurable
I am familiar with a number of
similar cases – irrespective of
their social background, their reaction to
terminal pain democratizes them.
Today I sat beside a dying Cockney
(detect a patronizing tone? – OK,
the living *ought* to patronize the dying):

> 'The wife was upset, as she's never seen
> me like this. So I said "We've all of us
> got to go, Girl, I've ad a decent life;
> it's im in the next bed as I feels sad for,
> e's only young – they ad to stop is pain
> by a-leucotomizing-of is brain."'

*　*　*

[He writes] *Dear* [names of the Managing Director and one of the editors of his publishers], *I am irritated to learn that I shall soon be dead. You will be irritated to learn that by then I shall have completed a final book. This epistle constitutes one of its 100 sections. I shall be dead by the time you receive this typescript. Set it in the old way – in Tedious Acrimonious roman and Poppa-Piccolino italic on hand-deckled ipeca-cuanha leaf bound in reversed brushed papoose.* [He signs his name.]

PS. Seriously, though, my wife will deal with proof correction.

*　*　*

105

[*Ubi sunt* the beldam who collapsed in Pride of Plaice, the micropalaeontologist with C. ventriculi, the hag carried off by ambulance from Azalea Terrace, the loon barbiturate ingester, the Master of the 100 100-Word Units, the C3 sniper victim, the lady with C. uterine cervix, the lady with breast cancer, the gent with bladder ditto, Epicurus, the jet-set exec-looking Head of Fine Art (snuff sternutator), the leucotomized folk-singer (singin whack for my diddle), &cⁿ? All planted, at the time of going to press. Some feared oblivion; most feared pain. Poor frail dear frightened little vulnerable creatures.]

* * *

so long as we exist death
is not with us;
but when death comes,
then we do not exist.
The diseases of my
bladder
and stomach are pursuing   [Pah.]
their course, lacking
nothing of their usual
severity; but against all
this is the joy in
my heart at the

I knew what I'd got, I'd
seen it in my notes,
looked it up in the
medical books, knew I
couldn't recover.
Wanted
to talk about it with
the doc but he always
seemed too busy, or just
called it inflammation.
Oh love, don't go, stay;
hold my hand, *tight*, love

* * *

I have administered anti-emetics and stool softeners and allowed him to eat and drink. He seems free of pain and nausea but vomits periodically whilst remaining comfortable. He describes the sensation as being similar to defecating – relieving an uncomfortable fullness. I treat his ascites with the insertion of a LeVeen shunt. Unfortunately he has developed fungating growths and draining fistulae. Particularly troublesome are the fistulae in the perianal area originating from the urinary and intestinal tracts. I performed Turnbull's Diverting Loop Transverse Colostomy (see *Current Surgical Techniques*, Schering, 1978). Bloody oozing, odour and haemorrhage occur from his decubitus ulcers.

* * *

My fistulae ooze blood and stink,
I vomit puce spawn in the sink,
diarrhoea is exuded.
Do not be deluded:
mortality's worse than you think.

You find the Limerick inapposite? Try the pretty Choriamb?

Bed-sores without; swarm-cells within.
Rancified puke speckles my sheets.
Faeces spurt out quite uncontrolled
into my bed, foetid and warm.
Vomit of blood tasting of brass,
streaked with green veins, splatters my face.

In vomiting, the glottis closes, the soft palate rises and the
abdominal muscles contract, expelling the stomach contents. In
nausea, the stomach relaxes and there is reverse peristalsis in
the duodenum.

* * *

The list goes on and on interminably . . .
Rectal Bleeding, Chemotherapy
('Oh, how I dread the fortnightly injection –
the pain of it *itself*, and after that
ill for a week from the after-effects.
Anger is what I feel at dying, *anger* –
why can't the dropouts and the drunks get This?
I've always led such a clean, simple life . . .'),
Mastectomy, Metastases, Dyspnoea . . .
the list goes on and on and on and on . . .
(Some die in agony of mind and body
described by Hospice staff 'Dehumanized'.)
'Grief Work', 'Death Work', smug 'Terminal Caregivers' . . .
         I close my eyes but weep under the lids.

                    * * *

Crystalline water I sipped a few moments ago is returned as
vomit of discoloured filth, swarm-juice of rank-cancered gut.

C is for cardiac illnesses also – nothing to envy:
someone in High Street drops dead, shoppers, embarrassed/
                                        thrilled, gawp.

I can now vomit with accuracy and certain discretion
into the steel kidney-bowl, hourly they clear the puked slime.

Someone, nocturnally, in the adjacent corridor, expires:
I hear a bloody great thud, then someone mutters 'Now, *lift*'.

I can no longer depend on my body doing my bidding;
ill bodies baulk at deep thoughts (of suicide and twee verse).

                    * * *

It is not as one can imagine beforehand. Dysgneusia (an altered sense of taste occasionally occurring in cases of advanced malignancy) prevents my savouring the cigar-box-spiciness, deep, round fruitiness of the brick-red luscious '61 *Cheval Blanc*, the fat, buttery, cooked, caramel-sweet-nuttiness of the 1894 Bual.

'He is a patient with dysgneusia and severe dysphagia and a fairly advanced tumour for whom adequate hydration and nutrition are maintained by frequent small feedings of liquids. The insertion of an intraluminal esophageal tube is considered helpful. The dysphagia is due to an obstruction in the esophagus and hypopharynx.'

* * *

An absorbent pad placed under the corner of the mouth at night will prevent dribbling causing wetness and discomfort. Ice may help stimulate muscle movement. Pass an ice cube from the corner of his mouth towards the ear, then dry the skin. It may help to wipe an ice cube round his lips, then dry them. (One of them had some movement in the eyelids and was able to blink Morse messages.) Phrase questions to receive very simple answers, e.g.: 'There is jelly and ice cream or egg custard – would you like jelly and ice cream?' Pyjamas should be absorbent.

* * *

Never had a husband. No one to care when it happened except Jesus. Pain. Radiotherapy. Terrible terrible pain. No one to care. Energy gone. Tired. So weak. Hair falling out. *Actually falling out!* Bald. Quite bald. The Good Book. Had to give me a wig, National Health – couldn't've afforded it myself. Always put my trust in the Lord. Never missed a Sunday. But now, somehow . . . Oh what will happen? Oh Gentle Jesus meek and mild oh Gentle Jesus help me *save* me Gentle Jesus the Good Book, *Revelation,* vi. 8. Of course Mr Tucker comes to help, a real help.

* * *

In Ashes Valley this evening I crawl under
      sheltering bushes
Joined at the same stock, so close together they
      let no light through them
And where no rain can pelt through their meshed roof, so
      knitted together
One with the other they grow. And I merge myself
      into the brown husks.
Weakly I rake together a litter from
      dry leaves that lie here
Deeply sufficient to succour two or
      three if they wanted
Warmth against Winter however malicious the
      elements' onslaughts.
Thus do I bury me closely with leaf-mould and
      wait for Athene's
Soft anaesthetic, benign soporific, ar-
      cane analgesic . . .

* * *

. . . by a vagrant.
There was an empty
bottle, and, oddly,
a glass and decanter
– rather posh ones.
There was no money.
Oh, yes, and this
page of note-pad . . .

final lines of the sestet
of the final Petrarchan.
'Hollow' forms the first
c. I require dcdee. 'Follow'
could be the second c.

No. Something more prosy
for this job. The morphine,
the colostomy – fuck-all
there is justify lyric/metre.
But some structure still?
Why? Dignity? – bollocks.

But some structure still,
incongruously . . .

100 units each of 100 words.
How about that? Neat. One unit
per day for 100 final days

* * *

Precambrian sub-division *Longmyndian*, ca. 600 million yrs. old. An individual Holocene *H. sapiens* with terminal pathogen. The co-incidence of these two, thus: approaching oblivion (by ingestion of soporifics), *H. sap.* picks up, from scree in Ashes Hollow, a sample of rock imprinted with 600-million-year-old rain-pits. Suddenly, alas, the subtle grafting of a cdcdee Spenserian sestet onto an abbaabba Petrarchan octave does not matter. Vita b.; ars b. Nor does the Precambrian sub-division *Longmyndian*, ca. 600 million yrs. old, nor Holocene *H. sap* with terminal &c., nor the *conception* of its not mattering, nor

* * *

(The suicide is untrue. Bodily weakness prevents my moving from the bed. The dismay to my wife and child which suicide would occasion renders such a course untenable. They would interpret my self-destruction as failure on their part to nurse me properly. Conversely, the grief my daily decline causes them is difficult for me to bear. If I could only end the terrible work and unpleasantness I cause them . . . But bodily weakness prevents my moving from the bed. Shit gushes unbidden from the artificial anus on my abdomen. My wife patiently washes my faece-besmirched pyjamas, for *prosaic* love.)

UKULELE MUSIC

Dear sir,

*I come in this morning instead of tomorrow as I have to take ~~Budige budgie~~
Bird to the Vets, as he got out of cage door for the first time, By <u>accident</u>. As
I was putting seed in. & taking out sand sheet. He went mad. & banged
himself against THE wall. & fell down on to the Magic coal fire. got
jammed in the back of coal effect. Broken leg and side of his body awfull
state. he is in. good job fire was not on.*

faithly Viv

*p.S. could you oblige the next weeks money this wk. be in tomorrow
Morning, Only the Capting which I chars for tuesdays has let me off this
Tues but has PAID yrs Viv*

'They must have been about 17/18, possibly 19:
one, tattooed on his hand MAM; one, tattooed on his arm LOVE.

One of them grabbed at my handbag but I just belted him with it,
caught him one under the ear, then I yelled "Somebody, help!"

Even although it was lunchtime and several people were
                                                    watching
nobody wanted to know. Two women just walked right past.'

She had been pushing her 8-month-old, Sharen-Jayne, in the
                                                    buggy.
Now the kid started to scrawk; one of our heroes smirked, spat,

fondled the empty pint bottle he had in his hand and then
                                                    smashed it
on an adjacent brick wall, held the bits to the child's throat.

'I said "Hurt me if you like but don't injure the innocent baby –
it can't defend itself, see? Don't do it don't do it *please!*"

He said "If I do the baby I'll get what I want, so I'll cut it."
He shoved the glass in her cheek; twisted the jagged edge in.

He told me "This is how we earn our living, this and the dole
                                                    like."
Then he just wiggled the sharp, smashed slivers into her eye.'

Promptly the mother gave over her golden wedding-ring, also
three pounds in cash and a watch (silver, engraved 'My True
                                                    Love'),

118

but the attackers slashed Sharen twice more – in the mouth, and a
deep cut
neatly round one chubby knee. Then they strolled leisurely off.

'Sharon was screaming and bleeding a lot and I thought they had
killed her.'

C.I.D. officers say 'This is a callous assault . . .'

Dear Sir,

will finish of your hoovering and such tomorrow as my hand is still bad, my right one. As last wk. there is a lady two doors off me has a bitch and a little boy over the road had been playing with it. and since then where all the dogs came from I do not know. But one of them had pinned the boy against the wall. I ran out with a hand full of pepper to throw at the dogs face. I throw it. but it had bit me in the hand. just above my right thumb where the bone is. I ran after the dog. with a whitening brush also and I fell also over the fence. bruised my knee's. But my knee is alright. My hand I have sufferd. The dog got put down to sleep. I have been to Hospitle But I heard later. that another dog had pinned the same boy he is only four yrs old. and MARLD him in the face and eyes he has had 5 stitches across his left eye. The other dog also had to be put down to sleep I tell you it has been awfull over there with the dogs. The woman who the bitch belongs to, had forgotten she had left her kitchen window open One of the dogs had jump in through the window. her Husband had delt with the dog. But slammed the kitchen window and all of the glass had fallen out in pieces. (It is awfull. when the little girls are about.) There mothers have to keep them in. or take them with them. the pain is going all the way up my arm. I have had a TECNAS. you know, a little RED CARD.

YRS Viv.

Someone has left a whole crateful of empty lemonade bottles
on the pedestrian bridge. Here come three ten-year-old boys.

Queuing for buses, the off-peak shoppers are gathered together
under the cast concrete span (aerosolled WANKERS and TREV).

Each of the children has picked up an empty and, quite
                                        nonchalantly,
hurls it down onto the grans, young mums and spinsters and
                                        babes.

No one evinces surprise or alarm or even vexation,
fox-trotting through the smashed bits, Terpsichorean and deft.

Each boy throws four bottles, spits from the parapet into our
                                        faces,
shouts 'Fucking bastards' and yelps. Glass crunches under a bus.

Blood smears the calf of an elderly lady silently weeping.
'Kids' our conductor observes 'should be done something about.'

Grans are bewildered by post-Coronation disintegration;
offspring of offspring of *their* offspring infest and despoil.

('You think you're doing a fine job of work don't you, oh yes, but
you're not. Stop it stop it, it's dirty dirty dirty in the streets like
that' an old woman shopper informs two boys of ten or eleven
who slouch against a butcher's window in busy Northcote Rd.,
SW11. Moist beige tripes gleam. Around the Chopper bikes blobs
of bubbly saliva streaked green and yellow describe a semi-circle
on the greasy pavement. The boys giggle and one of them remarks
sotto voce 'Fuck off old cow'. 'What did you say?' They giggle
and do not answer. One boy spits afresh at his colleague's cycle.
A glycerite sac depends from the canary-coloured spokes, elon-
gates gradually. 'Dirty little devils. Look at them look at them!'
she appeals to those of us nearby. We evince neither surprise nor
concern. She turns begrudgingly. Silver streaks jet concurrently
from gaps between the front teeth of each boy. She continues
upon her way unaware that her pink leatherette mac is sullied by
twin viscid drools.)

Stubbornly, Taffs, at their damn-fool anachronistic eisteddfods,
still, with this breach in the hull, twang (ineffectual lyres).

Mercury falls, it's no go, and the pink geraniums shrivel:
ceilidh and Old Viennese drone as the packet goes down.

When all the cities were felled by the pongoid subspecies in them
(Belfast, Jerusalem, Brum., Liverpool, Beirut) and when

blood-swilling (Allah is wonderful) Middle-East Yahoos had
purchased
nuclear hardware, he found distich the only form apt.

Too Many Of Us and Dwindled Resources and War had undone
us.
Matter impartially throve (quark, strangeness, charm) not as *us*.

Sing in Your Bath if You Want to Seem Sexy and **Blood-Bath
in Jordan**
vie for front page in the tabs. Doh ray me fah soh lah te

well, Sir

Only, the Capting has said I was not really wanted so I have gone to you instead. only. You are not here as you know. So have let myself in with spare key but he has PAY me just the same as he is kind old man with heart of gold etc. and has told me how underneath. and he has seen it with OWN eyes so knows it is true. where I thought it was just Underground Car Park ect. under ~~Civic~~ Civet Centre is not just Car Park but bunk for FALL if there is trouble, that sometimes seems likely with uSA and russiens with there bomb warfair. but what can you do? nothing and he say there are SARDINES stored in there for after siren. with DRINK. so we are all prepared thank God. But what I want to know is when you vote the different Goverments do NOT do what you ask do they? Because I want NO TROUBLE but it seems no difference what you want the Rulers just do a DIFFERENT THING. So you can only keep CHEERFUL and keep trying your best. sir. for Exsample I have done the floors but their is one of Yr writings there that ALAS is swept in the Hoover bag, and I got it out all right but is VERY twisted with the thing that BEATS as SWEEPS as CLEANS the one about a Piano and Man AND woman that I think is DIRTY but it takes all sorts and did you REALLY work at such a club in uSA? I never knew you had been there but I would not want sardines ALL THE TIME who would? noone. but it would be <u>emergency</u> like in the last one where it was tin sheeting. But now they are on the streets the ARMY against thugs and Mugers as that is where the REAL war is on NOW, cities in 2 halfs with police and army and nice folks against dirty animals, so may HAVE to go DOWN soon for THAT war. But I have throw it away, the poetry writing on the Piano at top of kitchin bin VERY TOP if you want it back.

and Oblige Viv.

Beetrooty colonels explain to the Lounge Bar how, in the 'Last
                                                          Show',
they had a marvellous time, and how we need a new war

if we are going to get this Great Country back on its feet, sir
(also all beards should be shaved: also the Dole should be
                                                          stopped).

Life still goes on and *It isn't the end of the world* (the child-soothing
platitudes weaken now Cruise proves them potentially false).

Lieder's no art against these sorry times (anguished Paramour
                                                          likens
mountainy crags and a crow to the flint heart of his Frau).

Dear sir,

have done some hoover of the front room. but am going now be back tomorrow morning if you can oblige with next week money same as last time. Only my sister. not the one in Australia the other one here. was standing at the bus station when boys threw bottles and ones broken glass flew up and cut leg BAD CUT. only about ten also, she says so must go and help as she is lost a husband recently too. I tell you no one knows how bad it is here with these children ALL OVER. They will be the death of us no mistake. also the world situation no better, America Russia jews and Arabians irish and such. what can you do as it gets worse like one of yr poetry Works that I saw when cleaning desk with wax which I need more of soon as possible please. The same as in the empty tin. but well what can you do only get on with it. as you can't sort it all out can you? we are like the man in music Hall song that goes he plays his ~~Uku uker~~ Youkalaylee while the ship went down. only we all have problems like my sister and Goverments so can only carry on best we can, the next weeks money this week please as am short due to various things and the new wax pollish Viv.

PS. doctor said it is not SO bad but has had 6 stitch.

126

Glossy black slices of smooth slab are all laid facing towards due
East – in the twerpish conceit sunrise might pleasure them *now*!

Glittery gilt lists the names and the dates and the bullshit about
>   them
– 'Fell Asleep', 'Gone to Rest' (tcha!), 'Resting in Jesus' Arms'
>   (pah!).

'Gone Where We'll All Join Again on the Happy Shore Everafter'
(spew, vomit, puke, throw-up, retch), 'Went Without Saying
>   Goodbye'.

Inside a shed with the Council's coat-of-arms blazoned on it
there is a Flymo and spades. Here comes a gent with a pick:

'Wouldn't it make you want to dip your bread in the piss-pot
– some of the bilge they write there? Fuckin daft sods' (he opines).

Sweet peas are cunningly wrought in a huge pink crucifix resting
fresh on damp just-replaced turf. Wet clay outlines a new slot.

Biro-smudged sympathy-cards blow about and one is signed
>   'Viv, The
Depest Regrett Always Felt' (it shows a wren on a wreath).

On a diminutive gravy-hued sandstone wafer is chiselled
that which, despite mawkishness, prompts a sharp intake of
>   breath.

Aged 10.
Little Boy,
We Would Not
Wake You To
Suffer Again.

Oh sir,

only I havnt known. which way to TURN since the Funeral. It was the sisters youngest such a good lad too and only ten it seems wrong. somehow, and they would play in the streets though they was told often enough GOD only knows. So it was a bus when they was playing football and the poor little mite had gone when they got him. to the Hospitle so that is why I didn't come for 3 days but was in this morning and hope you find this note behind the tea pot and with thanks for the new Polish which have done the desk and chairs with. My oldest Trevor has been TOWER OF strenth since tragdy but <u>will</u> get those tatoos just like his DAD in that way just last week got MAM done on his hand which is nice he is a good lad to his Mother and a Tower. So can I have last weeks moneys though I did not come and not have money next week instead. Only the flowers which was a cross of pink flowers. very nicely done. do cost such a lot not that you bigrudge it do you when its your own Sisters youngest? So if you could leave it buy the dusters and furnature wax it will be fine tomorrow.

Obliged, Viv.

PS we take her to the zoo next weekend to take her out of herself. the sister. as it will be a nice change our Trevor says.

'Them animals is disgusting.'

In London Zoo is a large flat painted Disneyesque lion
sporting a circular hole cut where the face ought to be.

On its reverse is a step upon which the visitor stands and
puts his own face through the hole – so that he may be thus
                                                                                    snapped.

So, the resultant photograph shows the face of a friend or
relative grinning like mad out of a leonine frame.

This seems to be a very popular piece of equipment –
Arabs in nightshirts and Japs queue with Jews. Polaroids click.

Tabloids blown underfoot headline a couple of global débâcles.
Gran, from the lion's mouth, leers: toothless, cadaverous, blithe.

Oh it is very funny to put your head through the facial
orifice of a joke lion – races and creeds are agreed.

Down the old Monkey House there is a *Cercopithecus* wanking
and a baboon (with its thumb stuck up its arse) to revile.

Dear Sir didnt come in yesterday as planned as I lost key and how it happened was this. that we went to zoo with sister and the children which was the sister lost her youngest. And while we was throwing a ten pence for luck onto back of Allergator corcodile which is in Tropical House it must have fell from my purse. Everyone throws money for luck onto back of this Reptille and his pool is FULL of two P ten P and 5P pieces which bring GOOD LUCK to thrower. So had to go yesterday to see if the keeper had found it. he had and said they empty pool every month and spend money. It buys keepers there beer he says they get POUNDS so I got key back that is why I am here today instead but unfortunatly have by ACCIDENT spoilt one of your papers with poetry on it that was on yr desk as I threw it on the Parkray by mistake. and hope this is no inconvenience or can you do another one instead? Sister much better since outing but oldest boy Trev in trouble with police who came last night to house but I dont believe it as he is a good boy. But she is perking up a bit now and was cheerful at weekend and my boy took a Poloid Photo of her with head through a LION which was V. funny and makes her laugh which is good for her. Police say he has mugged but it canot be as he is GOOD BOY.

faithly VIV. p.s. worse things happen at SEA!

'Life is too black as he paints it' and 'Reading's nastiness sometimes
seems a bit over the top' thinks a review – so does *he*.

Too black and over the top, though, is what the Actual often
happens to be, I'm afraid. He don't *invent* it, you know.

Take, for example, some snippets from last week's dailies before
they're
screwed up to light the Parkray: Birmingham, March '83,

on her allotment in King's Heath, picking daffodils, Dr
Dorris McCutcheon (retired) pauses to look at her veg.

Dr McCutcheon (aged 81) does not know that behind her,
Dennis (aged 36) lurks, clutching an old iron bar.

Unemployed labourer Dennis Bowering sneaks up behind her,
bashes her over the head – jaw, nose and cheek are smashed-in.

Dennis then drags her until he has got her into the tool-shed,
strikes her again and again, there is a sexual assault,

also a watch and some money worth less than ten pounds are
stolen.
'Is an appalling offence . . .' Bowering is told by the Judge.

Amateur frogmen discover a pair of human legs buried
Mafia-style in cement, deep in an Austrian lake.

Smugly, Americans rail over KA 007*;
angrily, Moscow retorts. Hokkaido fishermen find

---

* In September 1983 a Soviet fighter plane shot down a South Korean airliner when
all 269 passengers were killed, causing a brief stir.

five human bits of meat, one faceless limbless female Caucasian,
shirts, empty briefcases, shoes, fragments of little child's coat,

pieces of movable section of wing of a 747,
one piece of human back flesh (in salmon-fishermen's nets),

one headless human too mangled to ascertain what the sex is.
USA/USSR butcher a Boeing like chess

(probably civil jumbos *are* used for Intelligence business;
pity the poor sods on board don't have the chance to opt out).

Sexual outrage on woman of 88 robbed of her savings.
Finger found stuck on barbed wire. Too black and over the top.

Clearly we no longer hold *H. sapiens* in great reverence
(which situation, alas, no elegiacs can fix).

What do they think they're playing at, then, these Poetry Wal-
lahs?
Grub St. reviewing its own lame valedictory bunk.

dear Sir,

well I have hooverd and wax pollish the desk so I will collect money tomorrow. There is trouble on our block since my Tom plays the bones to tunes of George Formby and was due to give a TURN at the club tonight but was paralitic last night and WOULD try to practise and of course one of them. the bones. went over next door and the woman there that has the bitch that MARLD the child well her bitch grabs the bone but my Tom shouts abuse and. of course the outcome is there is a window broke. Which the man next door have only just mended after the last trouble. so we will see how it goes tonight at the Club he does that one he played his Youkerlaylie as the Ship Went down. and I know how He felt, because it is the same with my eldest Trevor who is REPRIMANDED IN CUSTARDY as the policeman put it who is a nice man but I know my lad is innerscent of that awful thing they say he done. But these things are sent to TRY Us as my Man says and I hope he plays his bones well tonight. just like he did that year we were in T.V. show Mr and Mrs, did you know we were in it? yes in Llandudno and he entertained the crowds they were in stitches when the ONE MAN BAND never turned up. so I have used up all the Johnsons Wax again so please oblige, We all have problems even the different Parlerments, also the police Forces. as well as me, and you with Yr writings.

Viv, P.S. we can only carry on the best we can manage

Down at the PDSA there's a queue of unprepossessing
buggered-up budgies and dogs. Someone is telling how Rex

quite unaccountably ('Never been known to act like it previous')
set on the nipper next door, and must now 'get put to sleep'.

'Even although he has done such a thing – and that to a kiddy –
I can't help loving him still – you *have* to stand by your own.'

'That's what I feels about my eldest (Trev) – they've done him for
                                                          mugging –
still, you *must* still love your own; if he's bad, he's *still* my boy.'

Cotton wool tenderly placed in a shoe-box comforts a frail life.
There is much love at the Vet's – even for bad dogs and Trev.

Was one time anchored in forty
fathom near unto the shore
of Mascarenhas Island.
Landed, we found blue pigeons
so tame as to suffer us
to capture them by our hands
so that we killed and roasted
above two hundred the first day.
Also we took many others –
grey paraquets, wild geese
and penguins (which last hath but stumps
for wings, so cannot fly).
Most entertaining to catch
a paraquet and make it
cry aloud till the rest
of its kind flocked round it and thus
enabled themselves to be caught.
Twenty five turtle, lying
under one tree, was taken.

On then to St Mary's Island,
where we careened, and thence
stood for the Straights of Sunda.

At 5° 30′
south of the line, the alarm
'Fire!' was raised – the steward
had gone below for brandy,
thrust candle into the hole
of a cask on the tier above
whence he drew his spirits, and when
removing his candle, a spark
had fell from the wick down the bung,
igniting the spirit. He poured
water unto the cask,

by which we had thought to choke it.

But the flames, reviving, blew out
the cask ends, when the fire
reached to a heap of coals
stowed there, which, lighted, gave off
a thick sulphureous smoke
thwarting attempts to extinguish it.

In this emergency
I appealed to the supercargo
to cast overboard all powder.
But (stubborn, arrogant, greedy,
as so many of his class)
he refused. Says he 'To throw
our powder away is to risk
attack from our enemies'.

Meantime the rage of the fire
augmented more and more.
We scuttled decks that greater
floods of water could be
got into ye hold, but all
attempts proved vain.

                I resolved
to summon the carpenters
with augers to bore the hull
that water might enter below
and quench the flames.

                But our oil
ignited then, d'ye see?,
and with sixty five good men
I stood on deck by the main

hatchway receiving buckets
when the powder, 300 kegs,
was reached.

        The vessel blew up
into the air with one hundred
and nineteen souls: a moment
afterwards, not one single
human being was seen:
believing myself to be launched
into eternity,
I cried out aloud for Mercy.

Some slender remnant of life
and resolution still lurked
in my heart. I gained the wreck,
as was gone to a thousand pieces,
clung to a yard.

        The long-boat,
got off afore the explosion
by a deserting faction,
now, in the very worst
of my extremity,
ran to the place with all speed,
whereat the trumpeter
threw out a line by which
I obtained that frail haven
of temporary ease,
and hymned being simply extant.

Cast up, one time, wrecked,
on bleak Patagonia
out of the Wager, Indiaman,
Commodore Anson's squadron.
Six years, afore we reached home.
Only food, shellfish and raw seal –
as we managed to stone unto death
or found dead, raw, rank, rotted.

Reduced thus to misery,
and so emaciated,
we scarce resembled mankind.
At nights in hail and snow
with naught but open beach
to lay down upon in order
to procure a little rest –
oftentimes having to pull off
the few rags I was left wearing,
it being impossible
to sleep with them on for the vermin
as by that time swarmed about them;
albeit, I often removed
my sark and, laying it down
on a boulder, beat it hard
with an huge stone, hoping to slay
an hundred of them at once,
for it were endless work
to pick them off one by one.
What we suffered from this
was worse even than the hunger.
But we were cleanly compared
of our captain, for I could compare
his body to nothing more like
an ant hill, so many thousand
of vermin crawling over it;

for he were past attempting
to rid himself in the least
of this torment, as he had quite
lost himself, not recollecting
our names that were about him,
nor his own. His beard as long
as an hermit's: that and his face
being besmirched of filth
from having been long accustomed
himself to sleep on a bag
in which he kept stinking seal meat
(which prudent measure he took
to prevent our getting at it
as he slept). His legs swelled huge
as mill-posts, whilst his torso
was as a skin packet of bones –
and upon bleached seal bones he played
hour after hour in uncanny
tattoo as to harmonize
with a wordless mindless dirge
as he moithered, moithered, moithered,
weird, xysterical airs,
yea, even unto the end.

Was one time cast on Oroolong,
when the Antelope packet went down.
The king of Coorooraa
succoured us, gave us meat,
in return of which we shewed him
the swivel as we had salvaged
out of the wreck, and the six-
pounder and our small-arms.
He and his natives were thrilled
and astonished. A flying squirrel
having settled upon a tree
nearby, our captain's servant
loaded his musquet, shot it.
Seeing the animal drop
off of a lofty tree's top,
without, apparently,
anything passing to it,
they ran to take it up;
when, perceiving the holes,
they chuckled, evidenced glee
and begged to be allowed
guns for themselves that they might
do slaughter of their near neighbours
whom they were desirous to see
fall, full of holes, as this,
dead in great quantity.
We acquiesced.

        They made
great execution with these,
our fire-arms, puzzling their foes,
who could not comprehend
how that their people dropped
without receiving any
apparent blow. Though holes

141

were seen in their bodies, they couldn't
divine by what agency
they were thus, in a moment, deprived
of motion and life. The whole
of the prisoners taken was shot.
We objected upon this last,
explained inhumanity
unto ye simple minds.

Their king gave unto us then
a kind of victory banquet,
whereat one tar of our number,
who out of the wreck had saved
an Italian violin
and had the bowing of it,
struck up. I know not whether
twas due to the victory,
or the feast, or to the grog
of which we allowed them a plenty,
or whether the fiddle musick;
but, be it whichever, they reeled,
cavorted like monkeys and fell
euphoric with our company
unto ye general dust.

Sailed one time aboard
trawler the Lucky Dragon,
crew o' 23,
hundred miles off Bikini,
in the March of '54.

Tars was all below
down in the a'ter-cabin;
crew man, Suzuki,
run abaft a-hollering
'The sun rises in the West!'

Hands mustered on deck,
saw, to larboard, a fireball,
like a rainbow brand,
rise up from ye horizon,
silent, that was the queer thing.

Minutes passed; the blast
suddenly shook the ocean,
shuddered our whole hulk,
hands was belayed with affright,
none, howsomdever, hurt (*then*).

But the skies turned *strange* –
misty wi' weird white ashes
as *swirled*, d'ye see?,
down onto decks, men, rigging . . .
That ash made us ill (*later*).

Most awful, terrific form
shipwreck can take is fire;
where the unfortunate
victims has only two
alternatives – to seek death
in one element in order
to avoid it in another.

One time the enemy's powder
(with whom we was close-engaged)
took fire – match left a-purpose
by their skipper, damn his eyes –
both the vessels blew up,
most violent dreadful explosion.

We, the spectators, ourselves
were the poor players also
in the bloody scene – some thinking
maybe it were the Last Judgement,
confounded, unable to gauge
whether or no we beheld it –
two ships hurled up on high
two hundred fathoms in air,
where there was formed a mountain
of fire, water and wreck;
dread conflagration below,
cannon unpeeling above,
rending of masts and planks,
ripping of canvas and cordage,
screams, like stuck pigs, of brent tars.

When the ship first took fire
I was blowed clean from the forecastle,
fell back into the sea
where I remained under water

unable to gain ye surface,
struggled as one afeared
of drowning, got up and seized
a bulk of mast as I found
nearby.

      Saw floating about
divers wounded and dead –
two half bodies, with still
some remnant of life, a-rising
and sinking, rising and sinking,
leaving the deep dyed pink.
Deplorable to behold
scores of limbs and fragments
of bodies – most of them spitted
on splintered timbers and spars.

Survivors we boarded a boat
almost entire from the wreck.
Most of us vomited constant
from swallowing pints of sea water.

I suffered long and swelled
to a surprising degree,
all my hair, face and one side
of my body were brent with powder;
bled at the mouth, nose, ears
(I know not whether this
be the effect of powder,
by swelling up the vessels
containing the blood of our bodies
to such extent that the ends
of the veins open and ooze it;
or whether it be occasioned
by the great noise and violent

motion in the same organs –
but let it happen which way
it will, there was no room there then
for consulting of physicians).

Thro the long night some sang,
attempting to keep up spirits.
Merciful Providence
preserving some measure of wine
and rum from the hold, the mate
contrived then to engineer
a musical instrument
on which he made bold to play.

Since I have so often felt
the malignant influence
of the stars presiding over
the seas, and by adverse fortune
lost all the wealth which, with such
trouble and care, I amassed,
it has been no source of pleasure
recalling to memory
the disasters that have assailed us.

Still, as a singer a song
or an old player an air,
I am impelled to convey
salt observations, a tar's
chantey habit, d'ye see?

I know not whether we've bid
adieu to the sea, or whether
we shall set forth again
where we have known such mischief;
whether traverse the ocean
in quest of a little wealth;
or rest in quiet and consume
what our relations have left us.

Our strange propensity
to undertake voyages,
alike to that of gaming –
whatever adversity
befalls us, we trust, at length,
prosperity shall o'ertake us,
therefore continue to play.

So with us at sea,
for, whatever calamity
we meet with, we hope for some
chance opportunity
to indemnify our losses.

And shall it, now, be counted
as ye dignified defiance
in us towards our fateful
merciless element,
or gull naiveté,
cousin to recklessness,
that, e'en in pitching Gulphward,
our salt kind brings forth chanteys?

Who would have thought it Sir, actually putting ME in a WRITING!
me and the Capting and ALL. What a turn up for the books.

Only, I must say I do not know HOW them people in poems
manage to say what they want – you know, in funny short lines,

or like what YOU do with them ones of yours sir, made of two lines like.
Still, when you're USED to it like, then you can speak natural.

Only, the newspaper man said that you was TRYING to sound like
low classes voices and that, only you wasn't no good –

you know, the CUTTING you left on yr desk top when I was waxing –
you know, that CRICKET which said you wasn't no good at all?

when you got TERRIBLE, stamping and raging calling him stupid
and how the man was a FOOL, which was the day you took DRINK.

'What is to one class of minds and perceptions exaggeration,
is to another plain truth' (Dickens remarks in a brief

preface to *Chuzzlewit*). 'I have not touched one character straight
                                                              from
life, but some counterpart of that very character has

asked me, incredulous, "Really now *did you* ever see, *really*,
anyone *really* like that?"' (this is the gist, not precise).

Well I can tell that old cricket that this is JUST how we speaks like,
me and the Capting and all (only not just in two lines).

One time, returning to home port, fell in with Englishman (16-
gunner) bound England from Spain; hailed her heave-to and
belay.

After a skirmish we forced her to strike her colours and seized
her.
Auctioned her off at Rochelle; carried the prize to Bordeaux.

Our tars had been so long absent from home that now we
indulged in
every extravagant vice, ere we be called to ye Deep.

Merchants advanced us, without hesitation, money and goods
on
promise of that which was our share of the booty, d'ye see?

We spent the night in whatever amusements best pleased our
fancy –
claret and gore and the stench of ye rank pox-festered trulls.

We spent the next day traversing the town in masquerade,
ranting,
had ourselves carried in chairs, lighted with torches, at noon.

As we caroused thus abroad we caused music, plucked forth
from gambas
boldly, t'embellish the raw, rude Dionysian debauch.

And the drear consequence of this gross wanton mass indiscre-
tion
was the untimely demise of damned near all the whole crew.

Jimmy 'The Beard' Ferrozzo, aged 40, Manager of the
Condor Club, where I now work (down San Francisco's North
Beach),

died when the stage-prop piano we used for Carol the stripper
pinned him tight into the roof, causing his breathing to stop.

Mr Boyd Stephens, the medical guy who did the autopsy,
said that Ferrozzo was pressed so tight he couldn't inhale,

said that 'Compression Asphyxia' is the name of the ball-game –
pressure had squashed up the chest so hard it couldn't expand.

I have been Caretaker down at the topless Condor Club now for,
must be a couple of years. When I unlocked, 9 a.m.,

I found Ferrozzo draped over his girlfriend (23-year-old
Trixie – this slag from the Club, nude Go-Go dancer, you know?).

She had no clothes on and she was stuck, screaming, under him
– it was
three hours before she could be freed by the cops from the raised

Steinway, a prop they have used at the Club for 2 decades almost
(topless star Carol descends, sprawled on the keys, to the stage).

Even now, no one knows what caused the joke piano to rise up
into the ceiling, 12 ft., pinning Ferrozzo and Trix.

Police say the motor that operates on the lifting device had
burned out and couldn't be switched so as to bring it back down.

Some way the Manager's body had kept her 2 or 3 inches
off of the ceiling and stopped Trixie herself being crushed.

Det. Whitney Gunther says: 'She was so drunk she doesn't
                                               remember
laying down nude on the strings inside the grand – she just
                                               knows

sometime that a.m. she woke up to hear the twanging of taut
                                               wires.'
Man! What an Exit, you know? Welter of plucked gut and spunk.

Only, because it has broke (I.T.V.) we HAD to watch 'Seasars' –
stories about the roam Kings, dirty disgusting old lot.

One of them dressed up in smelly old skins and rushed out at captives
wounding there PRIVATES with KNIFE. also had LOVED his own
                                               Mam.

this is called 'Narrow' which plays on a fiddle, all the time Roam burnd
but why it Brakes is because. my man has FIXED it last week

Also my mack is at cleaners because of kiddies which MARK it
ever so bad with their spit. They should be children of Roam –

what with the way they go on with their dirty, horrible, habbits
One of which made them all HEAR while he plays music all nite.

This one is known as 'Callegulum' which is v. funny name for
King but is THERE on t.v. So must be right. it is pink

leather effect with a belt and the reason why there is broken
glass on barometer is: cutting a LONG story short.

My man is playing it just as a banjo, being the SAME SHAPE.
singing the George Formby Song. and he has drop it on FLOOR.

SO that the glass and the silvery stuff you get in it all come
out and can not be got back. One of them SAWED men in half

also he has a poor soul stabbed to death with terrible pen nibs
also a mans' brains flogged out using a CHAIN for three days

which is the same sort of thing that you get in newspaper these days.
what with the Irish and that. so I have bought a new GAMP.

That is because of the Mack but he also made FATHER's go to
SEE their own kiddies killed dead, that was the worst thing of all

so it has broke and the needle now ALWAYS points to the STORMY –
he is a fool to have PLAYED (Formby) But ROAM is BAD TIME

Nero springs out girt in lynx pelts and slits slave's dick with a
                                                        razor . . .
ROAM is BAD TIME, as is Wolves: January '84,

19-year-olds Brian Johnson and friend Troy Blakeway are
                                                        jogging,
that they may catch the last bus, after a disco in town.

Leaving the Old Vic Hotel, Wolverhampton, they are pursued by
25 rampaging youths (West Indians, it appears).

Johnson leaps onto a bus but is stabbed twice just as the doors
                                                        close
(two deep long cuts in the thigh, 15 and 12 inches long).

At the Royal Hospital he receives more than seventy stitches.
Blakeway is knifed in the back, trying to flee from the mob –

in the deep 6-inch-long gash he gets thirty stitches; a sobbing
middle-aged parent attends (whose hand a nurse gently pats).

'Very sharp instruments must have been used for making these
                                                          nasty
injuries' C.I.D. says (Johnson and Blakeway concur).

It has not been without usefulness that the Press has adminis-
                                                          tered
wholesale mad slovenly filth, glibly in apposite prose,

for it has wholly anesthetized us to what we would either
break under horror of, or, join in, encouraged by trends.

Horrible headlines don't penetrate. Pongoid crania carry
on as though nothing were wrong. *Homo autophagous*, Inc.

**Gillian Weaver aged 22 walking 4-year-old daughter
home when a girl and three men** – hang on, this isn't just *news*:

Gillian Weaver aged 22 walking 4-year-old daughter
home when a girl and three men push her to pavement and steal

£3 from purse – she sits weeping and nursing 4-year-old (let's not
wax sentimental re kids; let's stick to facts, here *are* facts).

As she sits weeping and hugging her daughter, one of the
                                                          muggers
comes back and razors her thus **slashes her face 50 times**

(this is the *Mirror* and not my*self* – *I* have no axe to grind, right?)
C.I.D. seeks three blacks plus one spotty, ginger-haired
                                                          white.

Meanwhile, I've gotten the *5-Minute Uke Course* (Guaranteed
                                                    Foolproof) –
plinkplinka plinkplinka plonk plinkplinka plinkplinka plonk.

Grans are bewildered by post Coronation disintegration;
offspring of offspring of *their* offspring infest and despoil.

This is the Age Of The Greatly Bewildered Granny & Grandad,
shitlessly scared by the bad, mindless and jobless and young;

also the Age Of The Dispossessed Young, with nothing to lose by
horribly hurting their sires, babies and cripples, and whose

governments, freely elected and otherwise, function by mores
not altogether removed from their own bestial codes –

those sort of policies, that sort of hardware do not imply much
kindly respect for *H. sap*, mindless and jobless and young . . .

Maybe we're better off under the Civic Centre than up there
what with the LUTEing and that – them inner-cities is BAD,

maybe we're better off here in his WRITINGS, orrible though they
often is sometimes, than THERE – out in that awful real-life

what with its madness and sometimes I thinks the Capting's the only
sane one among the whole lot – Four or five leagues West-sou'west!

Steadily bear away under a reefed lug foresail, ye bilge rats,
synne rises firey and red – sure indycation o'gales,

we have entrapped us a sea-mew and served the blood to ye

weakest

members of crew, and myself? Liver and heart and ye guts.

For accompanying singing, the haunting harmony of the Uke has
no superior! Soft summer nights and the Uke are inseparable
pals! To wintry jollities the Uke adds zip and sparkle! Too much
mystery and confusion have shrouded Uke playing! The Uke is
an instrument for the best accompanying of happytime songs!
Beautiful and very unusual effects can be achieved! <u>You</u> can learn
to play richly harmonious accompaniments *in only a few minutes* by
this New Method, and when you have done that **you have
accomplished a great deal!**

'This is not Poetry, this is reality, untreated, nasty',
'This is demotic and cheap', 'This is mere caricature',

'This is just relishing violent, nasty . . .' so on and so forth,
Grub St. reviewing its own lame valedictory tosh –

*Don't you go brooding and brooding and getting all of a state sir
just cos the LITARY GENT don't seem to like your nice books.*

*Like the old man used to always say 'When we wants YOU to chirp-up,
matey, we'll rattle the cage' – don't heed their old tommy-rot.*

Grasp the pick lightly between thumb and first finger of right hand. Do not pinch! Move tip of pick back and forth across all four strings. Let that wrist hang loose! Start slow and then increase speed until you produce a smooth, even tone. Well done! The speed you move the pick across the strings will depend on what we call *tempo* (that means *time*) of the number you're accompanying! Well done! **That sounds just dandy!**

These are the questions that Councillors mean to raise at the
Meeting:
how much promethium remains? Has there been tritium used?

Why did the Army deny there was any contamination?
How do they mean to assure residents no risk remains?

What was the level of contamination? Where had it come from?
What is a 'low level' leak? Why was the public not told?

Why has the Army consistently issued flagrant denials
that any toxin remained after these secret 'events'?

Now you are ready for those oldies we know and love! Yes *Sir*!
Sing, hum, or whistle the tune as you play! Play each chord as indicated until a new chord is shown. Do not change until you see another chord indicated! Everyone's just <u>got to</u> join in and **sing right along there!**

Carrying on as though things were O.K. is what we are good at –
fall-out-proof bunkers are built, orbiting space stations planned.

Only, it's worse in the papers than what you stick in your writings, what with I seen a man knocked down WITH MY OWN EYES by black man and poor soul that was muged was ON CRUTCHES and that is gospel truth but not as bad as burning baby with CIG END which some swine done to get purse from mother of two. So even if they are out of work it is NOT RIGHT they should hurt their own townspeoples. Any road it is too late now so we can just HOPE FOR BEST which I DO, and will only live in shelter or outer spaces if there is no other possible. But will NOT eat sardines morning noon and night.

Finally now we return to the deep, and reaching our dim craft
drag her black hull through safe shale down to the fathomless
brine.

Next, to the dark-bellied vessel we carry white sails and main-
mast,
lifting aboard her the sheep, white tup and black ewe, and now,

heavily laden with misery, shedding tears in abundance,
hark to our skipper's command, nimble in wit and resource.

Thus we embark while astern of us rise up sail-swelling breezes
surging the blue-prowed ship forth, 12 knots with main-skysail
set.

So, d'ye see, after putting our gear and tackle in order,
all we can do is observe, course set by helmsman and wind.

Thus with full canvas we traverse the waters into ye blackness;
tenebrose, fog-bound, the bar, into the tow of the stream.

Here is perpetual smoke of a city unpierced by sunlight
where ye Cimmerians dwell, unvisible from above.

Here we make fast and drive up from the bilges, bleating, the
                                                        stunned sheep
into these bunkers of lead, granite and greyness and stench.

Wend your luff, messmates, and let go the skysail halliards,
                                                        mister,
cut the brace pennants and stays, reef the fore-topgallant in,

falling barometer, send down the skysail yard from aloft, sir,
strum with felt pick back and forth, lightly across all four strings,

all sail should be double-gasketted, stow the mainsail and cross-
                                                        jack,
make yr pentameters taut: two-and-a-half feet times two,

bend ye now three lower storm-staysails and a storm spanker,
                                                        mister,
take in the three upper tops, close-reef the foresail, F sharp,

tighten the B string and place finger at the back of the second
fret of the A string and keep spondees and dactyls close-clewed,

trim yr heroic hexameter (or it may be dactylic),
splice the pentameter aft, finger yr frets as ye go

surely we shouldn't be speaking like this sir, not in Allergic
Dis Talk, taint natural-like: I'm goin back to me prawse

only I've not been old self since they started the TREATMENT but do not
WORRY as they SWEAR it is non malingerent tumer ONLY which only
in my opinion only needs GOOD TONIC and will soon be old self again
but sometimes feeling bit on queer side that is to be expected the doctor say,
but what with one thing and another and the worry over eldest boy in trouble
with LAW I do not know which way to turn but I do wonder when you read
these cases what do the mothers think. and the father's. because they are all
some mothers children which loves them I should say. Even if they are vilent
crimnal. So will soon be back on feet again but this worry is worrying with
internashnal TROUBLE brewing as the BULLETIN says and I do not
feel so perky as previous. So will sign of for the present

if I could only be just this once pardoned Spawndies and Doctale
which we has never heard of down at the Ten-Storey-Flats.

The Triple Roll is one of the prettiest of all Uke strokes! It is a
very simple stroke too, when analyzed! Just follow the simple
stages below one step at a time! Soon you will get the 'knack'!
Yes, *Sir*!

Bring forefinger down across all four strings where neck joins
body of Uke. Bring that old fingernail down so that it glides
smoothly on the strings. That sounds just swell! Practise this
again and again and again! **Then follow with thumb down**.
After forefinger leaves last string bring ball of thumb down across
strings. **Then bring first finger up**. As thumb leaves last string,
bring the ball or fleshy part of forefinger up across all four strings.
Yes, *Sir*! Forefinger should begin to go up the very second that
little old thumb leaves the last string! Say! That sounds like a
million dollars! You, good buddy, have just mastered yourself the
TRIPLE ROLL!!!

I had believed myself fairly inured to foolishness after
6 months for Reuter's in parched mad bloody Lebanon, but

leaving the hotel that morning (with Dickie Pratt, of the *Mirror*),
in the main street of Sidon, I was presented with this:

out from the shade of the shelled former Admin. Offices stepped
a
miniature, wielding a huge glinting black muzzle and stock,

just as a fat juicy jeep of Israelis swung into vision.
Three or four seconds he stood, sputtering hail at the jeep –

windscreen-glass frosted and one of the front seat occupants
oozed red,
there was a crackle of fire, ten or so seconds, and then,

as from a colander, into the pavement streamed out the juices
of the assailant, a slight soldier/homunculus. Well,

nobody looks for a *motive* from these old Testament shitters –
thick hate is still in the genes. I learned the boy was aged 12.

Say! At the outset, the beginner may find his finger just a little bit
stiff and clumsy but this disappears quickly after a little practice!
So why not keep right on along gut-pluck-a-plickin come rain or
come shine! Yes *Sir*! Let's start with the **little finger down** where
the neck joins the body . . .

'Tries to be shocking', 'Predictable, coarse, insensitive,
tasteless . . .'
when I want you to chirp-up, matey, I'll rattle the cage.

Say! What you need to do each day is keep that little Uke in tune!
Yes *Sir*! Who wants to hear an out-of-tune Uke? That's right! –
Nobody! Say! Why not tune that Uke right now? O.K. let's go!
You need a piano to help you. Tune A string to A on piano. Tune
D string to sound the same as D on piano. Tune F-Sharp string
and B string to sound like those notes on piano. Get it? If you do
not know where these notes are located on piano then ask some
guy who's a pianist to show you. Right?

What with the waiting and not knowing what on earth is the matter
up in the cities and that. Still, it was awful up there

what with last Wednesday that one what married him from the Top Flats
pushing the babby she was, down by the Preesint new shops,

suddenly found erself total surrounded by what-do-you-call-em?
them Rasterfastium blacks; you know, the ones with the LOCKS.

One got er purse but the pleece come and then the LEADER a FAT man
snatched up the babby and STABBED – right in the EYE with a pen,

animals that's what I think of them monsters horrible wild BEASTS
not safe to walk in the streets – not that we could NOW, of course

only it's funny for us being down here under the Civict
Centre – I thought it was all Underground Car Parks and that.

During this voyage ye heavens has been so dree overcast that
no observation by stars, nor yet by sun can be got.

Little round light like a tremulous faint star streams along
                                                    sparking,
blazes blue, shoots shroud to shroud, running along ye main
                                                    yard,

stays half the night with us, settles on fore-shrouds. Spaniards
                                                    call it
Fire of St. Elmo – be damned! Fire of ye Devil, it be.

Only the Capting gets mixed up about his time in the Navy –
muddles it up with them YARNS. You know, them ones what you READ,

not as I'm one for the books and that what with doing the housewort
(no Womans Libbance for ME, what with that much things to do.

get on with THIS Viv and THAT Viv and, well you has to LIVE don't
                                                    you?
that's what I think, any road). Close-clew your sails, mates, avast,

shew a reefed foresail to steer by and run for harbour my buckoes,
oakum discharged from hull's seams; pipe up all hands to the
                                                    pumps!

Make ye now ready for Davy Jones, messmates, get ye the
                                         strings tuned,
highest grade sheep's gut, they be – list to the boatman, belay,

as o'er the stream we glide borne by the rolling tide chanting and
                                         rowing . . .
Place your 3rd finger behind 3rd fret of 4th string and strum

Only I've never been happy but what I'm pottering, I ain't –
always the pottering sort, that's why I hates coming DOWN

mind you the Powertree Bloke and the Capting doesn't arf GABBLE –
what with the Capting his YARNS: tother keeps chaingin is VOICE

anyone'd think they was Everyone All Times Everywhere, way they
gabbles and rambles and that: still, they can't help it, poor souls.

Whatsisname says to me 'Viv you're the life and soul of the party' –
Viv, he says, MEANS life, you know (in Greek or Lating or French)

p̄linkp̄linkǎ|p̄linkp̄linkǎ|p̄linkp̄linkǎ|p̄linkp̄link|p̄linkp̄linkǎ|
                                         p̄linkp̄link
p̄linkp̄linkǎ|p̄linkp̄linkǎ|p̄lonk‖p̄linkp̄linkǎ|p̄linkp̄linkǎ|p̄lonk